To:

My Friend

From:

Ben Davis

Date:

5-9-23

Be Blessed!

Every Day with God

Copyright © 2019 by Christian Art Kids,
an imprint of Christian Art Publishers,
PO Box 1599, Vereeniging, 1930, RSA

© 2019
First edition 2019

Designed by Christian Art Kids
Images used under license from Shutterstock.com

Printed in China

ISBN 978-1-4321-2947-7

19 20 21 22 23 24 25 26 27 28 – 10 9 8 7 6 5 4 3 2 1

Printed in Shenzhen, China
November 2018
Print Run: 100403

EVERY DAY WITH GOD

CHERIE HILL

CHRISTIAN ART PUBLISHERS

To Blaine and Bodie

Praying that you will know that
when you look for God every day...
you WILL find Him.
He is with you ALWAYS!

Daddy and I love you.

CONTENTS

For Times When...

How to use this devotional:

Are you ready to go on a fun, faith-filled adventure with God? Well then, this is how you can get started:

Step 1. For the first 5 days of the week read:
- A Scripture verse from the Bible.
- God's personal message to you. Yes, that's right. Each devotion is written as if God Himself is speaking to you.
- An awesome prayer for you to pray to God. It is the perfect way to end every devotion.

Step 2. On Saturdays it is time to recap on those key Bible verses you read during the week. Short, easy-to-read summaries of each verse will guarantee that you truly understand and remember God's special word for you.

Step 3. Sundays are perfect for reflecting on the treasures that you've discovered that week. So grab your pen and start journaling your thoughts and feelings about the exciting truths you've uncovered in God's messages for you.

You are now ready to start your amazing adventure with God!

Look to Me

I pray that God, the source of hope, will fill you completely with joy and peace because you trust in Him. Then you will overflow with confident hope through the power of the Holy Spirit.

Romans 15:13

— o — ~~~ — — o —

When life is hard...when things aren't going your way and you feel frustrated, know that I have a plan to give you hope. When you feel like you cannot trust anyone else, trust Me and the promises I have made you.

Above all else you are My child and I have promised you good things for your future. When you're down, look up...I AM with you always—hope in Me is all you need.

Lord God, help me to hope in You. Fill my heart with Your love and help me to have peace when life seems too hard for me.

Amen.

Focus on Me

Put your hope in the LORD.

Psalm 37:34

- o - ∿ - - o -

Life is not always going to go the way you want it to, but know that it will always go according to My perfect plan. You won't always understand My ways, and at times you will question and doubt My love for you because things are just not going right. But I love you more than you can imagine and I only want good things for you.

I want you focusing on Me, instead of all that you think you want and need. It's during the hard times that I will draw you near to Me, I will hold you close and give you peace. I AM all you need and I will fill your heart with hope.

Heavenly Father, I feel as though all hope is gone. Things aren't going right and I need You. I pray that You fill me with Your peace and teach me to hope in You alone.

Amen.

Believe in Me

Whoever believes in Him will not be put to shame.

1 Peter 2:6 (ESV)

— o — ∿ — — o —

I know that faith in Me is hard. You can't see Me and you can't hear Me in the ways you think you should. But one day, you will see Me face to face, in the way you want to. It's until then that I want you to just believe.

I will give you all you need each day if you will trust in Me for those things you desire. It may not always seem like I AM with you and you will often feel like you're alone, but you're not. I AM with you always...I will not disappoint you...just believe.

Heavenly Father, help me to believe in You even though I can't see You and hear You in the ways I want to right now. Give me hope to seek You more.

Amen.

Keep Praying to Me

Why, my soul, are you downcast?
Why so disturbed within me?
Put your hope in God, for I will yet
praise Him, my Savior and my God.

Psalm 43:5 (NIV)

— o — ∿ — — o —

You might feel helpless and things might seem hopeless, but everything is okay. I AM with you and I have the power to work miracles in your life. I can do the impossible. So, don't be sad, don't give up, keep trusting in Me and My promises for you...I will give you hope.

Hope is not gone when your hope is in Me. I hear every prayer you pray, I know all of your thoughts of fear and anger, and I know every tear you cry. Don't give up, nothing is too difficult for Me. Look to Me, keep praying to Me, and hold on to hope...no matter what.

Lord, help me to hold on to hope in You.
Help me to trust that You can do anything.
Give me peace that You are with me.

Amen.

Know That I AM in Control

"I know the plans that I have for you, declares the LORD. They are plans for peace and not disaster, plans to give you a future filled with hope."

Jeremiah 29:11 (GW)

$- \circ - \sim\sim\sim -- \circ -$

Life might seem overwhelming, like nothing is going right and things are not going to get better, but that is not what I have promised you. I have promised to give you peace and fill you with hope in your life. You won't always be able to control the things in your life, but you need to know that I AM always in control.

The most important thing is that you listen to My Word and follow My instructions for your life. It will not always be easy, but My Spirit is within you to help you do what you think is too hard to do. Trust that I have good plans for you and keep looking to Me for all that you need...especially hope.

Heavenly Father, I put my hope in You. Help me to trust that You have good plans for my life and I can rest in You.

Amen.

TIME TO REFLECT

When You Need Hope...

You will trust in God's promises to give you hope
and to encourage you as you wait patiently
for God to fulfill His promises in your life.

ROMANS 15:13

You will put your hope in the Lord.

PSALM 37:34

You will believe in God and be assured that
you will not be disappointed.

1 PETER 2:6

You will not allow your soul to be disturbed,
but you will put your hope in God and praise Him.

PSALM 43:5

You will trust in God's promise that His plans
for you are to have peace and to give you
a future filled with hope.

JEREMIAH 29:11

What I've learned this week about hope ...

_____

_____

_____

_____

_____

_____

_____

_____

_____

_____

_____

_____

_____

_____

_____

_____

_____

_____

Let Go and Let God

Give your burdens to the LORD,
and He will take care of you.

Psalm 55:22

- o - ∿∿∿ - - o -

When life isn't making sense, when you're confused and upset, I want you to just "let go" and let Me handle all that is bothering you. I want you to think about the things that are good—those things that make you happy.

I want you to stop when you're upset and know that I AM bigger than what is bothering you. I want you to enjoy your life and let Me deal with the hard stuff. I want you to give your troubles to Me and to just "let go."

Lord God, I am restless and I need You. Please calm me and help me to know that You have everything under control and everything will be okay.

Amen.

Trust in Me

"I know the plans that I have for you, declares the LORD. They are plans for peace and not disaster, plans to give you a future filled with hope."

Jeremiah 29:11 (GW)

— o — ∿ — — o —

Whether it's little things or big things, I need you to come to Me and trust Me. There is nothing too small and nothing too hard for Me. Though your frustrations in life may be hard for you to handle, I can do anything. I can fix what you can't. I do not become smaller just because your problems become bigger.

I may allow hard times in your life, but when you trust Me, your faith will grow and you will learn that I AM more real than you could ever imagine. When you are weak, I AM strong. So, thank Me for all I've done and all I'm going to do. When you're happy and when you're sad, know that I AM with you...*in everything*.

Lord, I trust You. I am going through a hard time and I need Your help. Please let everything turn out okay.

Amen.

Hold On to My Promises

When I worried about many things,
Your assuring words soothed my soul.

Psalm 94:19 (GW)

— o — ∿ — — o —

When you're feeling angry and unhappy with the way things are going in your life, I want you to trust that I AM all you need. I've made promises to you in My Word, the Bible, that you can count on.

I want to give you peace, so that you don't have to worry and so that you can enjoy your life. Don't be afraid, I AM with you and I've promised you good things. There is no reason to worry, no need to be upset...I want you to enjoy the life I've given you, by trusting in the promises I've made to you.

Heavenly Father, I am thankful for Your promises that comfort me when I am struggling with my feelings. Please fill me with Your peace when I am upset.

Amen.

Turn to Me

"Don't let your hearts be troubled.
Trust in God, and trust also in Me."

John 14:1

— ο — ∿∿ — — ο —

When you're in trouble, I know it makes you angry and afraid. I AM here to assure you that, no matter what, I love you and I will help you through your troubles.

Sometimes you get in trouble because of something you've done...sometimes it's because of what someone else has done, but it will be okay...whatever it is...I can fix anything. Keep praying to Me about all that is worrying you and know that I AM listening and I will help you in times of trouble.

Lord God, help me to come to You when I am in trouble. Help me not to be afraid and to know that You love me, no matter what. Fill my heart with peace as I trust in You to help me.

Amen.

Pray to Me

Don't worry about anything; instead,
pray about everything. Tell God what you
need, and thank Him for all He has done.

Philippians 4:6

- o - ∿∿ - - o -

I know sometimes you don't think that I hear you when you pray to Me. But I hear everything. I hear your heart and I know everything that you're thinking and feeling.

So when you feel all alone, when you're worried about all the things in your life that aren't going right, just pray to Me...ask Me for what you need and be thankful for all of the good things I've done in your life. Be thankful for the little things just like you are thankful for the big things. Be thankful, be grateful, and watch all the wonderful things that I will do in your life.

Heavenly Father, thank You for all of the blessings You have given to me. Teach me to be grateful for the good and bad things in my life, knowing that You are always in control and have good things planned for me.

Amen.

TIME TO REFLECT

When You're Upset...

You will give your burdens to the Lord,
and He will take care of you.

PSALM 55:22

You will trust that God
has good plans for you
and will give you hope.

JEREMIAH 29:11

You will not be anxious
or overwhelmed and you will turn to
God to comfort and encourage you.

PSALM 94:19

You won't let your heart be troubled.
You will trust in God.

JOHN 14:1

You won't be anxious
about anything. You'll pray and
be thankful that God hears you.

PHILIPPIANS 4:6

What I've learned this week about feeling upset...

_____

_____

_____

_____

_____

_____

_____

_____

_____

_____

_____

_____

_____

_____

_____

_____

_____

_____

_____

I Will Be with You

Don't be afraid. Just stand still
and watch the LORD rescue you today.

Exodus 14:13

- o - ∿∿ — - o -

Come to Me when you are afraid. I AM here to give you peace and let you know there is nothing to fear. I AM always in control and I have good things planned for you. So, if things seem confusing and life is too hard and scary, know that I AM always with you...

I will protect you and give you peace. I need you to trust Me and not be afraid.

God, sometimes I don't know what to do and I am filled with fear about what is going to happen in my life. I need You to fill me with Your peace so that I can rest, knowing that You are always in control.

Amen.

Know That I'll Protect You

When I am afraid, I put my trust in You.

Psalm 56:3 (NIV)

- o - ~~~ - - o -

There will be times when you will feel afraid. It may be because you just don't understand what is going on in your life, or because things aren't going very well and it seems like things are bad and out of control.

If you are feeling afraid, I just want you to pray to Me and focus on Me, instead of your fears. I want you to trust in all of the promises that I've made to you in the Bible. I have promised to always love you and protect you. When you are afraid...it's time to trust Me and know that everything is okay because I AM God.

Lord, there are so many things that happen in my life and I often feel afraid. I don't know what to do and I am scared. Please help me to know that You are with me and will help me with all of the things that make me afraid.

Amen.

I'll Fight for You

This is what the LORD says: Do not be afraid!
Don't be discouraged by this mighty army,
for the battle is not yours, but God's.

2 Chronicles 20:15

– o – ～～ – – o –

Sometimes it might seem like you are in a battle... you feel like things in your life are too hard and you have to fight all of the time. And then when things are tough, you want a way out and you feel like I'm not helping you.

There is no reason to feel down or afraid, I will help you when you look to Me to fight your battles for you and trust that I will always do what is good for you. It won't always be easy, but I AM bigger than anything...just trust in Me.

Heavenly Father, help me not to be afraid. There are so many things in my life that make me feel scared... help me to trust in You to always take care of me.

Amen.

Trust in My Love for You

Such love has no fear, because perfect love
expels all fear. If we are afraid, it is for fear of
punishment, and this shows that we have
not fully experienced His perfect love.

1 John 4:18

— o — ∿ — — o —

I know that you are not perfect, but My love is. I want you to understand My grace...it's a gift to you. So no matter what you do, I still love you. You don't have to do everything right...I love you even when you do wrong.

I just want you to come to Me when you know you've done wrong things...I don't want you to be afraid. My love for you is bigger than anything and I promise that nothing can separate you from My love.

Lord God, thank You that I can be assured that You love me, that I have nothing to fear and that when I am afraid, You will fill me with Your peace.

Amen.

I Will Make You Strong

The fear of the LORD is the beginning of wisdom,
and knowledge of the Holy One is understanding.

Proverbs 9:10 (NIV)

— o — ∿ — — o —

Feelings can be hard to deal with. They can get mixed up and make things seem worse than they actually are. Feelings can be really powerful and hard to control, but I want you to know that if you are afraid, it is not a feeling that comes from Me. The Spirit I have given you is a spirit of power, love, and self-control.

So when you are feeling afraid, I want you to use your self-control and remember that your fear is coming from the devil who is trying to trick you into not trusting Me. I want you to keep seeking Me when you are afraid and know that I will make you strong inside and give you peace.

Heavenly Father, my feelings make me so
confused and afraid. Help me to always look to
You and trust You when I don't know what to do.

Amen.

TIME TO REFLECT

When You're Afraid...

You will stand still and
look to God to rescue you.

EXODUS 14:13

You will trust in God.

PSALM 56:3

You will not be afraid or discouraged, because
you know that God will fight your battles for you.

2 CHRONICLES 20:15

You will trust in God's love
for you and not be afraid.

1 JOHN 4:18

You will remember that if you fear God,
you don't need to fear anything else.
Because when you trust in God, He will give you
wisdom to make good decisions.

PROVERBS 9:10

What I've learned this week about feeling afraid...

_____

_____

_____

_____

_____

_____

_____

_____

_____

_____

_____

_____

_____

_____

_____

_____

_____

_____

Give It to Me

Casting all your cares [all your anxieties, all your worries, and all your concerns, once and for all] on Him, for He cares about you [with deepest affection, and watches over you very carefully].

1 Peter 5:7 (AMP)

- o - ~~ – - o -

You need to know that I AM always watching over you, so you don't need to worry. I want you to trust that I will always take care of you and there is no reason for you to be upset or worry about anything.

I want you to rest, knowing that I AM always in control and I can fix all of your problems—big and small. All you must do is pray...talk to Me about what is bothering you. I will listen and help you to have peace while I work on fixing all the things you're worried about.

Lord God, I am giving You everything that makes me worry. I want to trust You to take care of my problems...big or small...and be at peace, knowing You are watching over me.
Amen.

DAY 23

I'm with You

Even though I walk through the [sunless] valley
of the shadow of death, I fear no evil, for You
are with me; Your rod [to protect] and Your staff
[to guide], they comfort *and* console me.

Psalm 23:4 (AMP)

─ o ─ ∿ ─ ─ o ─

I want you to know that I AM always with you. I
AM always watching over you, always hearing your
laughter, and always drying your tears.

I know what you want, and I know all that you need...
know that I can do anything, but I need you to trust
Me and get to know Me better. I want you to rest,
knowing that no matter how bad things might seem,
I AM in control and can make all of the bad things
turn to good.

Lord, when my life seems hard and nothing is going right,
help me not to worry, but to trust that You can take
all of the bad things and use them for good in my life.

Amen.

Hope in Me

There is surely a future hope for you,
and your hope will not be cut off.

Proverbs 23:18 (NIV)

− o − ∿ − − o −

I know it sometimes seems like hope is gone, like nothing is ever going to go right, but I've promised to give you hope. Worrying won't make things better...but praying to Me to help you will.

You can win over your worries by hoping in Me and all that I've promised you. Know that I AM always looking over you and always taking care of you. If you are looking to Me and believing all that I've promised, you will always have hope.

Dear God, I need to know that there is always hope, even when everything is wrong and nothing seems to be getting better. Fill me with Your peace, so that I do not worry.

Amen.

Have Faith

God is with you in everything you do.

Genesis 21:22 (NIV)

- o - ~~~ - - o -

When you are worried, I know it makes you afraid... which causes you to do things and say things you shouldn't. I always want you to have faith...no matter what. You won't always feel like having faith, so you will need to read the Bible, My Word, to give you peace, hope, and strength.

I AM with you in everything, I AM bigger than anything, do not worry—do not be afraid. Choose to have faith...not fear.

Lord, I get worried because sometimes I feel so alone.
I want to trust You. Please give me the faith I
need to hope in You at all times and in all ways.

Amen.

Think Good Thoughts

Don't worry.

Psalm 37:1

- o - ∿ — - o -

It's easy to just think about the things that are hard in life, the things that aren't going right in your life, instead of just thinking about Me. When you're not focused on Me, it causes you to think wrong thoughts, which only makes you worry more.

I want you to always be thinking of good things, always be praying, and make the decision to stop worrying. Know that I know your heart is hurting and I will wipe away every tear you cry. I want you to rest in Me and know that I will always help you...I love you and everything is going to be okay.

Heavenly Father, help me to think of good things and to focus on You, so that I do not worry. I need You to give me peace and certainty that everything is going to be okay.

Amen.

TIME TO REFLECT

When You're Worried...

You will give all of your worries to God and know
that He cares for you and watches over you.

1 PETER 5:7

You will not fear because God is protecting you,
guiding you and comforting you.

PSALM 23:4

You will trust that God will give
you hope for the future and not take
away the hope you have now.

PROVERBS 23:18

You will be at peace knowing that God
is with you in everything you do.

GENESIS 21:22

You will choose not to worry.

PSALM 37:1

What I've learned this week about worries...

_____

_____

_____

_____

_____

_____

_____

_____

_____

_____

_____

_____

_____

_____

_____

_____

_____

_____

_____

Find Rest in Me

"Come to Me, all who are weary and heavily burdened [by religious rituals that provide no peace], and I will give you rest [refreshing your souls with salvation]."

Matthew 11:28 (AMP)

— o — ⁓ — — o —

Life can make you tired. You can get tired from having fun, or you can get tired from things in life being hard—like when you are getting in trouble, or things aren't going well with your friends or family. I want to give you rest.

I've promised to give you rest, if you will trust in Me to take care of all of your problems. I AM able to take care of anything...so trust Me to help you rest, even when you're afraid—know that I will work all things together for your good.

God, I feel tired and I want to rest. Help me to be at peace in knowing that You are always with me to take care of me in every way, so that I can rest.

Amen.

Take a Break

We who believe are entering that place of rest. As God said, "So I angrily took a solemn oath that they would never enter My place of rest." God said this even though He had finished His work when He created the world.

Hebrews 4:3 (GW)

- o - ∿ - - o -

Sometimes it might seem like you never get a break, you are always busy doing things—sometimes it's fun—sometimes because there are things that have to be done that you don't want to do. I know you need a break—time to rest and just be at peace.

You will need to make time to be alone, to make the world quiet, and just spend time with Me...just Me and you. I want you to remind yourself to focus your thoughts on Me when you are worried. I will fill you with strength, peace, and hope. If you will give your troubles to Me, I will give you rest.

Lord God, I come to You so that I can shut the world out and find quiet time. Help me to be still and just spend time with You.

Amen.

I Will Help You

"I am the vine; you are the branches. Those who remain in Me, and I in them, will produce much fruit. For apart from Me you can do nothing."

John 15:5

— o — ∿ — — o —

I AM here to help you all the time, whether your problems are big or small. You need Me and you need My help because I can do anything.

I want you to rest and have peace even when life is hard. I want you to trust Me when you don't understand and stay connected to Me by praying to Me and reading My Word, the Bible. You don't need to worry, you don't need to be upset, angry or afraid. I AM always with you, always protecting you and always using all of the troubles in your life to make something good.

Lord God, I want to trust You more and not be worried, upset, angry or afraid. Help me to know that You are always using the bad things in life for good.

Amen.

I Will Give You Strength

Those who entered His place of rest also
rest from their work as God did from His.

Hebrews 4:10 (GW)

– o – ∿∿ – – o –

There will be days when you are just tired. You might not have any energy to even have fun like you want to. When things in life are really hard or you're really worried, it makes you feel tired inside. So, when you are feeling tired and weak, come to Me and I will give you rest.

When you're tired, feeling like you are not yourself and need help, come to Me and I will help you to have peace and strength, so that you won't be tired anymore.

Heavenly Father, I am feeling tired and weak, and
I need You to give me strength, so that I can
do the things I need to do. Help me to come to
You when I am tired, so that I can rest.

Amen.

Trust Me and Rest

He is before all things, and
in Him all things hold together.

Colossians 1:17 (NIV)

– o – ⁓ – – o –

Sometimes you just need to let things go, so that you can have peace and rest. I want you to trust Me to handle the things that you can't. You won't always understand things in life...most of the times things won't make sense at all. But, I've given you faith so that you can trust Me and rest.

I know you have a lot of questions, but I want you to try to let those go. I want you to just trust in My promises to you and know that everything is going to be okay because I AM God and I'm bigger than anything. When things feel like they are falling apart, know that I AM the One who holds everything together.

God, help me to always know that no matter how
hard things are and how impossible they seem,
You are above all and are always in control.

Amen.

TIME TO REFLECT

When You're Tired...

You will go to God and let Him carry your burdens,
so that you can rest and He can refresh your soul.

MATTHEW 11:28

You will go to God to help you rest and
trust in Him to help you in every way.

HEBREWS 4:3

You continue to trust God to take care of
you and stay connected to Him in prayer.

JOHN 15:5

You will remember that you need to rest like
God rested when He created the world.

HEBREWS 4:10

You will remember that
God is bigger than anything and you
can trust Him to always be with you.

COLOSSIANS 1:17

What I've learned this week about taking time to rest...

_____

_____

_____

_____

_____

_____

_____

_____

_____

_____

_____

_____

_____

_____

I Will Make You Strong

Search for the LORD and for His
strength; continually seek Him.

Psalm 105:4

– o – ~~~ – – o –

When life is hard, it can make you feel so weak and tired that you don't even want to pray. I know it's hard and you need strength. I can help you. Just come to Me—especially when you're tired and weak.

When you don't know what to do—pray. When you're sad or mad—pray. I AM here to help you... to give you strength and give you peace...I AM with you always.

Lord God, I want to be strong, knowing that You are with me and that I don't need to be afraid. Help me to trust You and pray.

Amen.

I Will Strengthen You

The LORD gives His people strength.
The LORD blesses them with peace.

Psalm 29:11

There is always going to be trouble in life. There will always be things that make you afraid, but I AM always with you to give you the strength you need to make it through hard times.

When you're not sure you'll make it, when life just seems too hard, come to Me so I can give you more strength and fill your heart with peace. You can be strong and have hope because of all the promises I've made you. Just trust me to love you and take care of you—just have faith.

Heavenly Father, I need Your strength when I'm feeling weak. Help me to hope in Your promises to me.

Amen.

Wait for My Power

Yet, the strength of those who wait with hope
in the LORD will be renewed. They will soar on
wings like eagles. They will run and won't become
weary. They will walk and won't grow tired.

Isaiah 40:31 (GW)

— o — ⌇⌇⌇ — — o —

I always need you to stay focused on Me. It might not seem fair a lot of times, but you can always be sure that I will use all things—even the bad things—to create something good. Just because you don't understand things and it doesn't seem like I'm there...I have promised I AM always with you.

You don't always need to be strong...you can come to Me for help and I will make you strong. If you are waiting and nothing is changing...keep waiting on Me...trust that I will help you.

Father in heaven, I pray that You will help me to be strong when I feel like life is too hard. Help me to trust You when I'm weak and I'm not sure what to do.

Amen.

Find Courage in Me

"This is My command—be strong and courageous!
Do not be afraid or discouraged. For the LORD
your God is with you wherever you go."

Joshua 1:9

- o - ~~~ - - o -

I AM telling you to be strong. I AM with you and there is nothing to fear. You must choose to be strong when life gets hard. There is nothing you can't do if I AM helping you. There is nothing that I can't do—I do the impossible.

You need to know that I AM full of surprises! I hear every prayer you pray and I will answer you. I need you to wait on Me, be strong, and know that I AM with you.

Lord God, sometimes I feel very sad and discouraged.
I need Your Spirit to fill me so that I can be strong
when I'm afraid of what is going on in my life.

Amen.

Be Still

"Only in returning to Me and resting in Me will
you be saved. In quietness and confidence is your
strength. But you would have none of it."

Isaiah 30:15

− o − ∿∿ − − o −

You might think that if you are strong that you are taking control and doing things to fix problems in your life; but being strong sometimes means being quiet, seeking Me and trusting Me to work things out for you.

I will always give you direction, always help you to have faith to do what I ask you to do, and be with you each step of the way. There is nothing to fear, rest in Me, trust in Me, and I will give you strength.

Lord God, I need Your peace so that when I am having a hard time, I can be quiet and seek You. Help me to hear Your voice and know that You will tell me what to do.

Amen.

TIME TO REFLECT

When You Feel Weak...

You will search for the Lord and for His strength;
you will continually seek Him.

PSALM 105:4

The Lord will give you strength.
The Lord will bless you with peace.

PSALM 29:11

God will give you strength as you wait with
hope in the Lord. You will soar on wings like
eagles. You will run and won't become weary.
You will walk and won't grow tired.

ISAIAH 40:31

You will be strong and courageous!
You will not be afraid or discouraged. For the Lord
will be with you wherever you go.

JOSHUA 1:9

You will rest in God and be saved.
Quietness and confidence is your strength.

ISAIAH 30:15

What I've learned this week about strength and quietness...

_____

_____

_____

_____

_____

_____

_____

_____

_____

_____

_____

_____

_____

_____

_____

_____

_____

_____

I Offer Help in Trouble

God is our refuge and strength,
always ready to help in times of trouble.

Psalm 46:1

— o — ∿ — — o —

There will always be troubles in your life—some that you create, and some that you don't. I AM with you through them all. When life gets too hard, I know it can make you question if I'm real and if I really care about you. But just because life doesn't make sense, doesn't mean you should stop believing.

You must keep believing, no matter what. The ways I answer your prayers and help you can happen suddenly, or take time. So, I need you to be patient, keep praying and know that I will help you.

Father in heaven, I need to trust You more.
When I am in trouble, I need Your strength.
Help me to know You are always with me.

Amen.

Keep Believing

We are hard pressed on every side, but not crushed;
perplexed, but not in despair; persecuted, but not
abandoned; struck down, but not destroyed.

2 Corinthians 4:8-9 (NIV)

- o - ∿ - - o -

Sometimes it might seem like life is just too hard. You might feel like I'm not fair and that I don't care. But I've promised you that no matter how things look, I AM always working everything together for good.

Don't be afraid when you have problems in your life. Your problems give you a chance to come to Me, pray and get closer to Me, and allow Me to show you the miracles I can do in your life. Keep your eyes on Me and keep believing.

Lord God, I feel like so many things in my life are not going right. I don't know what to do and I need Your help so that I don't lose hope in Your promise that things will get better.

Amen.

Know That Hard Times Don't Last

"In this world you will have trouble.
But take heart! I have overcome the world."

John 16:33 (NIV)

– o – ∿ – – o –

I know there comes a time when life is just too hard and you need it all to stop. Just know that sometimes I allow problems in your life to draw you nearer to Me, to make you trust Me more—to make your faith stronger.

When you are frustrated, I want you to come to Me, thanking Me for all of the good things in your life—be thankful—even when life is hard. These hard times won't last, I've promised you that I will end them, just trust Me and be at peace.

Father in heaven, I am going through a really hard time right now and I need Your help. Help me to trust in You and know that things will get better soon.

Amen.

I AM Closer to You Than Ever

Why, LORD, do You stand far off? Why do
You hide Yourself in times of trouble?

Psalm 10:1 (NIV)

- o - ∿ - - o -

You might feel as though you are alone and in the dark, but I AM your light. Your faith grows when you have to trust Me during hard times and you have problems that are bigger than you.

Though you can't see Me, I AM with you always. Don't trust your feelings, only trust Me and all that I've promised you. There is nothing in your life that I can't fix. I make all things new. Right now, when you're afraid, I AM closer to you than I've ever been.

Heavenly Father, I feel so alone. I know that I need to trust in You, but it is hard when the things in my life are not going right. Give me peace to know that You are always with me.

Amen.

Call on Me

"When they call on Me, I will answer;
I will be with them in trouble.
I will rescue and honor them."

Psalm 91:15

- o - ~~~ - - o -

There is nothing for you to be afraid of—I AM bigger than anything. Your troubles might be too big for you, but nothing is too big for Me—and I AM with you always.

I will protect you and care for you and I will always be there to help you. Don't stop believing just because things don't change right away. I AM always with you to help you. I want what is best for your life—to give you good things. Just call on Me, know that I will answer, I will help you in times of trouble.

Dear God, I need help believing that You always hear me, that You are always with me and that You will always help me when I'm in trouble.

Amen.

When You're Having Problems...

You will turn to God as your refuge
and strength because He is always
ready to help in times of trouble.

PSALM 46:1

You will trust that although you are hard pressed
on every side, you will not be crushed;
though perplexed, you will not be in despair;
though persecuted, you will not be abandoned;
though struck down, you will not be destroyed.

2 CORINTHIANS 4:8-9

You will remember that God has said
that even though you have troubles,
He has already overcome them all.

JOHN 16:33

You will know that God is with you
even when He seems far away.

PSALM 10:1

When you call on God, He will answer
you and rescue you from your troubles.

PSALM 91:15

What I've learned this week about troubles and problems...

_____

_____

_____

_____

_____

_____

_____

_____

_____

_____

_____

_____

_____

_____

_____

_____

I Will Keep You Safe

No weapon that has been made
to be used against you will succeed.

Isaiah 54:17 (GW)

- o - ∿ - - o -

It's easy to feel like everyone and everything is against you—sometimes that might be true. But there is no reason to fear, I am with you to protect you and keep you safe and sound.

So if friends aren't nice, if you're feeling scared of things around you, remember that I have promised to stand up for you and to protect you. Nothing can get in the way of My love for you. You are always safe in My arms.

Lord God, I need to know that You will protect me and keep me safe and sound.

Amen.

I AM Your Rescuer

My eyes are always on the LORD, for He
rescues me from the traps of my enemies.

Psalm 25:15

— o — ∿ — — o —

When you are afraid, you first need to come to Me.
I AM always with you to help you. My Word, the
Bible, can keep you from being afraid if you trust
that I've promised to love you and protect you.

I will rescue you from the bad things in life, but
sometimes you must wait because My plan can take
time—so I need you to have faith and believe in Me
even when it's hard.

Heavenly Father, when I need You to protect Me
and rescue Me, I will pray to You and trust that
You are with Me and will do all that You've promised.

Amen.

I Will Guard Your Heart

The peace of God, which transcends all
understanding, will guard your hearts
and your minds in Christ Jesus.

Philippians 4:7 (NIV)

– o – ∿ – – o –

I realize that sometimes your sadness makes it feel like your heart is breaking. Know that I know about every tear that you cry. I don't want you to lose hope or give up when life is hard. I want you to come to Me and know that I will protect you and guard your heart.

Come to Me when you are sad and afraid—pray to Me—talk to Me like a friend and know that I hear you. Give Me your heart and I will guard it and comfort you—I will give you peace.

Lord, I am so sad, but I know that You are with me. Please take my heart and keep it safe. Comfort me with Your love.

Amen.

Rest in My Shadow

Whoever dwells in the shelter of
the Most High will rest in the
shadow of the Almighty.

Psalm 91:1 (NIV)

– o – ⌇⌇⌇ – – o –

I know that when you are sad or afraid you need to know that I AM with you to protect you. And I know that since you can't see Me, it is hard to believe. That's why I've given you the Bible, My promises to you, so that you can learn to have faith and trust Me.

You should know that I've promised to shelter you and to protect you. Even if bad things happen to you, I AM always with you and will one day make all of the bad things good. Come to Me and I will shelter you—you can rest in My shadow.

Lord God, help me to rest and know that You will be with me and protect me. Help me to have greater faith in You.

Amen.

Take Up My Shield of Love

Let all who take refuge in You rejoice. Spread Your
protection over them. For You bless the godly,
O LORD; You surround them with Your shield of love.

Psalm 5:11-12

– o – ⌇⌇⌇ – – o –

There will be times when life is so hard that everything will seem dark and scary and lonely, but you
must remember that I AM always with you. Even
when hope seems gone, it is not because it is
hopeless. I can do anything...all you must do is
trust in Me.

You are my child and I will always watch over you
and love you. I want you to come to Me when
you're in trouble or afraid. My love is a shield for
your heart, to give you peace at all times.

Dear God, help me to have peace and joy, even
when life is hard and I'm worried and afraid.
Help me to trust You more and more.

Amen.

TIME TO REFLECT

When You Need Protection...

You will trust in His promise that no weapon that has been made to be used against you will succeed.

ISAIAH 54:17

You will keep your eyes always on the Lord, for He will rescue you.

PSALM 25:15

You will allow the peace of God, which is far greater than we can understand, to guard your heart and your mind.

PHILIPPIANS 4:7

You will find shelter in the Most High and rest in God Almighty.

PSALM 91:1

You will take refuge in God and praise Him, because God has promised to surround you with His shield of love.

PSALM 5:11-12

What I've learned this week
about God's protection...

_____

_____

_____

_____

_____

_____

_____

_____

_____

_____

_____

_____

_____

_____

_____

_____

_____

DAY 57

Trust That I AM in Control

"For as the heavens are higher than the earth,
so are My ways higher than your ways and
My thoughts than your thoughts."

Isaiah 55:9 (ESV)

I know that when life is hard, you can get very confused. You don't understand why I don't do certain things or do them at a certain time and way. But you can't understand because you aren't able to see the big picture like I can. So, you must trust Me.

Don't let yourself give in to bad thoughts, getting frustrated and angry trying to control things that you can't control. Only I can control everything. I need you to trust in My ways and know that I will always do what is best for you. I'm full of surprises—just keep believing in Me.

Lord God, help me to be at peace knowing that You have everything under control and You know what is best.

Amen.

I AM Here to Help You

"In that way, you will be acting as true children of your Father in heaven. For He gives His sunlight to both the evil and the good, and He sends rain on the just and the unjust alike."

Matthew 5:45

– o – ∿ – – o –

I don't want you to stop believing in Me just because life gets hard and bad things happen. I AM with you during the good things and the bad. I know that when you're afraid or sad and things aren't getting better, you don't know if you really believe in Me. But you must keep believing.

This is how your faith grows. I need you to believe most when things get really hard. You can't just believe when life is easy. Come to Me always—I'm waiting for you.

Heavenly Father, thank You for the good things You give and thank You for helping me with the hard things in life.

Amen.

Know That I Will Bless You

"Test Me in this way," says the LORD of Armies.
"See if I won't open the windows of heaven
for you and flood you with blessings."

Malachi 3:10 (GW)

– o – ∿∿ – – o –

Life is full of things that don't go the way you want them to. Sometimes friends can hurt your feelings or decide not to be your friend anymore. But don't get discouraged.

Don't let yourself think bad thoughts. I want you to know I AM with you and you need to trust Me to bless you, to give you good things—to bring good things from bad. You need to keep believing that I AM in control and I will always help you and do what is best for you.

Heavenly Father, thank You for all of the ways
that You bless me. Help me to trust in You
and believe in You for bigger things.

Amen.

I Will Give You Peace

They were all terrified when they saw Him.
But Jesus spoke to them at once. "Don't be afraid,"
He said. "Take courage! I am here!"

Mark 6:50

– o – ∿∿ – – o –

There are so many things in life that can go wrong. Sometimes it will seem like nothing is going right. It's when things are really hard that you need My peace and rest.

I need you to pray when you're afraid, trust Me when you don't know what to do, and believe in Me even when you're not sure you should. When you pray, I listen, and I answer you. There is nothing to be afraid of, I AM with you, you can be at peace and rest.

Lord God, all I need is You. Help me to be at peace and have rest, knowing that You are with me in the good times and the bad.

Amen.

DAY 61

Get to Know Me Better

They strengthened the disciples in these cities and
encouraged the disciples to remain faithful.
Paul and Barnabas told them, "We must suffer
a lot to enter God's kingdom."

Acts 14:22 (GW)

– o – ∿ – – o –

I know you have lots of questions. You want to know
"why" things happen and "why" things are the way
they are. I know it's hard to believe in Me when you
just don't understand. But I have given you faith,
so that you can be strong and believe, even when
you're confused about life.

Sometimes you will understand what I AM doing,
but most of the time you will not. I want you to learn
to pray to Me, I want you to know Me better so that
your faith will grow stronger.

Lord God, please strengthen me and help me to
have faith even when I don't always understand.
Thank You for always loving me and helping me.

Amen.

TIME TO REFLECT

When You Need to Believe...

You will trust that God's ways are better than yours and you will believe Him no matter what.

ISAIAH 55:9

You will know that you are God's child and He loves you and is in control.

MATTHEW 5:45

You will trust God to open the windows of heaven for you and flood you with blessings.

MALACHI 3:10

You will not be afraid and know that Jesus is with you.

MARK 6:50

You will remain faithful and believe in God even when things are hard and confusing.

ACTS 14:22

What I've learned this week about having faith and believing...

_____

_____

_____

_____

_____

_____

_____

_____

_____

_____

_____

_____

_____

_____

_____

_____

Cling to Your Faith

I trust in Your word.

Psalm 119:42 (NIV)

- o - ∿∿ - - o -

Believing in Me won't always answer all of your questions in life. You will always have questions and there will always be hard things you have to face. That's why you need faith. Faith helps you to keep believing in Me, even when you're confused.

And faith has nothing to do with your feelings because you will always have problems that will make you feel like not believing in Me anymore. You must always believe what I've promised you. Go to the Bible, My promises, when you're confused.

Heavenly Father, when I have questions
and I'm confused, help me to keep believing
in all of Your promises and to be at peace.

Amen.

DAY 65

Believe My Faithful Promises

Take the sword of the Spirit,
which is the word of God.

Ephesians 6:17 (NIV)

— o — ⁓ — — o —

The world is filled with lots of lies. And lies will always hurt you and others. My promises to you, the Bible, will always help you when you are confused about life and not sure what to do.

Every day, every moment, you will need Me. And I AM always with you, always ready to help you. It is very easy for the devil to trick you and lie to you when you are confused, so I need you to always talk to Me and pray to me when you don't know what to do.

Lord God, thank You for Your Word, the Bible,
which is Your promises to me...so I can have
peace and hope when life is hard.

Amen.

Follow My Instructions

God gives wisdom, knowledge, and joy
to anyone who pleases Him.

Ecclesiastes 2:26 (GW)

- o - ~~ — - o -

I know it's not always easy to believe in Me and do the things you know is right. But doing what you know is wrong will really make you feel bad inside. And I want you to be filled with joy.

You will have joy when you come to Me when you're confused and pray about what you should do. Always follow My instructions for your life in the Bible, and I promise you I will fill your heart with peace and joy.

Dear God, thank You for always being with me
to help me to believe even when I'm afraid.

Amen.

My Spirit Will Help You

"The helper, the Holy Spirit, whom the Father, will send in My name, will teach you everything. He will remind you of everything that I have ever told you."

John 14:26 (GW)

When you believe in My Son, Jesus, I place My Spirit in you. He lives in you at all times. When life is hard and you're confused, the Spirit within you will help you and guide you when you are tempted to lie or do something you know is wrong.

It won't be easy, but you don't have to be afraid. I will always give you the strength to do what is right, but it will not always be easy.

Lord, thank You for Your Spirit within me that makes me strong and helps me to believe, even when it's hard to.

Amen.

Find Blessings in the Bible

God blesses the one who reads the words of this prophecy to the church, and He blesses all who listen to its message and obey what it says, for the time is near.

Revelation 1:3

– o – ∿ – – o –

Often you feel let down, like nothing is going right. It seems like you're always failing, like you can't do anything right, and you want to give up, but I AM here to help you when you're confused and upset.

I've given you My Word, the Bible, to reach your heart through the promises I've made in it. Everything you read in the Bible is meant to teach you My ways and My heart. So, when you're confused and need help, open the Bible, read the words and My Spirit will fill you. I will bless you in so many ways.

Lord God, thank You for Your Word, Your promises to me, and thank You for blessing me with Your peace and love.

Amen.

TIME TO REFLECT

When You're Confused...

You will trust in God's word.

PSALM 119:42

You will take the word of God
and trust it completely.

EPHESIANS 6:17

You will trust God to give you wisdom, knowledge,
and joy as you give your life to please Him.

ECCLESIASTES 2:26

You will rely on your Helper, the Holy Spirit,
to teach you everything you need to know.

JOHN 14:26

You will read the Word of God and obey
it, so you can be at peace and rest.

REVELATION 1:3

What I've learned this week about being confused...

I AM in Control

Let the heavens rejoice, let the earth be glad;
let them say among the nations,
"The LORD reigns!"

1 Chronicles 16:31 (NIV)

- o - ∿ - - o -

Most of the time life will feel out of control, but it is not—I AM always in charge. No matter what is happening in your life, you can be sure that everything is going to be okay.

It might sometimes seem that I'm not keeping My promises or I don't care about what is happening in your life, but I will always keep My promises and take care of you. Trusting Me won't always be easy, but you must keep trusting Me so that I can bless you in all the ways you need Me to.

Heavenly Father, at times I feel out of control...
like I can't control my feelings and I get really upset.
Help me to run to You when I'm feeling this way.

Amen.

I Will Fill You with Blessings

"My people will be filled with
My blessings," declares the LORD.

Jeremiah 31:14 (GW)

- o - ~~~ — - o -

There will be things in your life that make you so angry and upset that you lose control. You may even feel like hurting others because you are hurting so badly.

But when you're feeling this way, I want you to pray to Me and ask Me to help you calm down so that you can hear My Spirit within you...telling you that everything is going to be okay. I will bless you, I will take care of all that is making you afraid and upset.

I want you to have peace and know that I AM always in control, and I will always help you.

Lord God, help me not to lose control, even when I'm hurting and angry. Please fill me with Your peace so that I can be calm and trust in You to always help me.

Amen.

Know That I Will Never Leave You

All authority comes from God, and those in positions of authority have been placed there by God.

Romans 13:1

— o — ∿ — — o —

I know that you sometimes think I AM in control of some things, but not others. But nothing happens in the whole wide world without Me being in control over it all.

There is nothing in your life that I don't know about. I know all the things that make you happy and everything that makes you sad. So when things seem out of control, remember that I've promised to never leave you. And I've promised to always help you. Remember that I AM always in control...so you don't have to be.

Dear God, when things are out of control, please calm my feelings and help me to know that You are always in charge, so I don't have to be worried or afraid.

Amen.

I Will Fill You Up With Peace

The LORD will guide you continually, giving you water when you are dry and restoring your strength. You will be like a well-watered garden, like an ever-flowing spring.

Isaiah 58:11

- o - ∿ - - o -

When you get angry, upset, and even throw a tantrum, you are going to feel empty—I want to fill you up and give you peace and joy, even when things in your life aren't going right.

You need to come to Me and pray and listen, so that I can help you know what to do. I will give you strength when you're weak. And when you're tired and empty from life being so hard, I will fill you up with My peace.

Lord, I need You to give me strength when I'm weak and fill me with peace when I'm tired and empty.

Amen.

Pray and I Will Answer You

The highest angelic powers stand in awe of God.
He is far more awesome than all who
surround His throne.

Psalm 89:7

− ο − ∿∿ −− ο −

At times you forget who I AM. I AM all-powerful, the Creator of the Universe, Lord of all. I AM your heavenly Father and all that I AM, all that I do is beyond awesome.

I want you to have peace and joy, knowing that I AM your God and I can do anything. Keep praying to Me, I always hear you and My answers to your prayer will be nothing less than awesome.

Heavenly Father, thank You for reminding me of all
that You've promised me, and reminding me too
that You are above all, awesome in every way.

Amen.

TIME TO REFLECT

When You Feel Like Your World Is Out of Control...

You will rejoice and be glad
because "the Lord reigns!"

1 CHRONICLES 16:31

You will be at peace because God
has promised to bless you.

JEREMIAH 31:14

You will remember that all authority comes
from God and He is always in control.

ROMANS 13:1

God will always guide you and
He will give you strength.

ISAIAH 58:11

You will remember how awesome God is
and He can help you with anything.

PSALM 89:7

What I've learned this week about when things seem out of control...

_____

_____

_____

_____

_____

_____

_____

_____

_____

_____

_____

_____

_____

_____

_____

_____

Look to Me for Joy

When he arrived and saw what the grace of God
had done, he was glad and encouraged them all to
remain true to the Lord with all their hearts.

Acts 11:23 (NIV)

It's okay to feel sad. There will be things in life that make you feel alone and like life is just not fair. I AM here for you when things aren't going right and you're not sure if things are going to get better.

I want you to have joy every day. Even on the days when you don't feel full of joy, you can still have joy because I AM God and I will give you hope.

Lord God, help me to have joy every day,
even though sometimes I don't feel joyful.
Help me to look to You for my joy.

Amen.

Wait on Me to Answer

O Lord my God, You have performed many wonders for us. Your plans for us are too numerous to list. You have no equal. If I tried to recite all Your wonderful deeds, I would never come to the end of them.

Psalm 40:5

— o — ∿ — — o —

When you're feeling sad, I want you to remember that not only have I promised to always be with you, but I've promised to give you a future and a hope.

You should know that I spend time thinking about you. I know all of the things that make you sad. It's not always easy to wait on Me to answer your prayers, especially when you're really sad. Keep praying and keep being glad that I will do wonderful things in your life.

Heavenly Father, help me to always trust You, to wait on You, and to know that You can do miracles.

Amen.

Hold On to the Rock

The LORD lives! Thanks be to my rock! May God,
the rock of my salvation, be glorified.

2 Samuel 22:47 (GW)

— o — ⌇⌇ — — o —

There are always going to be a lot of things that change in your life and I know that life is hard when things change. But I want you to be still and be strong...I will give you strength. Just keep believing in the promises I've made you.

I will help you to be calm. I just need you to be thankful for all I've done for you and look forward to all that I will still do. No matter how crazy life is...I AM your Rock.

Lord God, thank You for being my Rock, keeping me calm and at peace, knowing that You will always help me and protect me, and give me joy in knowing You.

Amen.

Never Give Up

Since we are surrounded by so many examples of faith, we must get rid of everything that slows us down, especially sin that distracts us. We must run the race that lies ahead of us and never give up.

Hebrews 12:1 (GW)

— ○ — ∿ — — ○ —

When you look around, you will see things that make you sad and even mad, but when you look up, you'll see Me. I AM always with you, when nothing is going right, when you're feeling worried and not sure that you believe in Me in anymore.

Just choose to be glad, choose not to be sad, keep praying and never give up.

Dear God, remind my heart that all I need to do is pray and not give up. Help me to trust that You are with me and I should not be afraid or worry.

Amen.

I AM All You Need

The LORD is my shepherd; I have all that I need.

Psalm 23:1

— o — ∿ — — o —

You may think you need a lot of things, but all you really need is Me. Don't get too worried about what you do or don't have. Just be thankful and glad for today—for right now.

There is no reason to worry...there's no reason to be upset or sad. Like a shepherd that leads and cares for sheep, I will lead you...showing you what you should do. I will care for you in every way, so you don't have to worry. I will give you all you need.

Lord God, I sometimes feel like I need more, like I don't have enough. Turn my heart and eyes to You... to remember that I have all that I need if I have You.

Amen.

TIME TO REFLECT

When You're Sad...

You will remember the grace of God and be encouraged to keep believing and remain true to God with all of your heart.

ACTS 11:23

You will focus on the many wonders God does and know that His plans are for hope. You will be thankful and know that God's goodness will never end.

PSALM 40:5

You will give thanks to God, your Rock. You will trust Him to help you.

2 SAMUEL 22:47

You will get rid of anything that keeps you from having faith in God...especially the wrong things you do. You will keep focused on God and never give up.

HEBREWS 12:1

You will be at peace, knowing that the Lord is your shepherd and you truly have all that you need.

PSALM 23:1

What I've learned this week about feeling sad...

Listen and Search

They listened eagerly...They searched the Scriptures day after day to see if Paul and Silas were teaching the truth.

Acts 17:11

— o — ∿ — — o —

Having a relationship with Me is the most important thing in your life. I want you to pray to Me about everything and listen for My answers. Sometimes the answers will be easy, at other times it will be hard to know what to do.

I want you to keep searching for My answers. Don't give up when things are hard. I can do really amazing miracles when things are really bad. So keep looking to Me, I will always help you.

Heavenly Father, help me to listen for Your voice in my heart. Strengthen me when things are hard and help me to keep believing no matter what.

Amen.

Pray for Help

"Be strong and very courageous. Be careful to obey all the law My servant Moses gave you; do not turn from it to the right or to the left, that you may be successful wherever you go."

Joshua 1:7 (NIV)

— o — ∿ — — o —

To obey Me means to listen to what I tell you to do in the Bible. It's not always easy to do all that I ask you to do. When you're angry or upset, it's even harder to do the right thing, so you need to always pray to Me as soon as you're confused and not feeling right inside.

It is very important for you to be strong, brave, and careful to obey Me. When you feel like things aren't going right, remember I AM with you always to help you and give you hope.

Lord God, I come to You praying for help. At times, I just don't know what to do and I need to know that You are with me and that I don't need to worry.

Amen.

DAY 87

Look to Me

He who has compassion on them will guide them
and lead them beside springs of water.

Isaiah 49:10 (NIV)

- o - ∿ - - o -

When you have to decide between right and wrong, I need you to pray to Me and sit quietly with Me. I love you and I always want what is best for you, but you must make your relationship and time with Me the first priority in your life.

Look to Me, listen to Me, and trust Me, even when life is confusing and doesn't make sense. I will always work all things together for good.

Heavenly Father, thank You for Your compassion, the love You give me and how You always take care of me. Help me to always put my relationship with You first in my life.

Amen.

Come Alive in Me

Teach me Your ways, O LORD, that I may live
according to Your truth! Grant me purity
of heart, so that I may honor You.

Psalm 86:11

— o — ∿ — — o —

When you decide to believe in Me, I put My Spirit in you. I AM alive in you. It's through the Bible that you learn about Me and what is right and wrong. It's My Spirit in you that will remind you of all that I've taught you in the Bible.

When you pray to Me, when you don't know what to do, I have promised to strengthen you, make you wise, and always help you in all the ways you need Me to.

Lord, teach Me how to live the life You want me to and help me to always remember that You are alive in me.

Amen.

Discern between Truths and Lies

All Your words are true;
all Your righteous laws are eternal.

Psalm 119:160 (NIV)

– o – ∿ – – o –

Sometimes it's really hard to tell what is the truth and what is a lie. Things and people in the world can be very tricky. That's why I've given you the Bible and My Spirit within you so that I can help you.

If you've done something wrong...come to Me. If you're confused by what is true and what is a lie... come to Me. I will always help you to see the truth and I will always lead and guide you to make the right decisions.

Heavenly Father, thank You for the Bible that helps me to know what is the truth and what is a lie. Help me to always seek You when I don't know what to do.

Amen.

TIME TO REFLECT

When You Don't Know What To Do...

You will listen to God's voice through the Bible.

ACTS 17:11

You will be strong and courageous, and
you will be careful to obey God.

JOSHUA 1:7

You will be thankful for
God's compassion and
praise Him for always guiding
you and leading you.

ISAIAH 49:10

Thank God for teaching you how He wants you to
live your life so that you will be blessed by Him.

PSALM 86:11

You will not fear and you will turn
to God's Word that is truth.

PSALM 119:160

What I've learned
this week about times when
I don't know what to do...

_____

_____

_____

_____

_____

_____

_____

_____

_____

_____

_____

_____

_____

_____

_____

Just Ask

You don't have what you want
because you don't ask God for it.

James 4:2

- o - ~~ -- o -

I always want to help you, but you need to ask for My help. I hear every prayer that you pray. I know every tear that you cry. I know when you are tired and frustrated and I can give you peace in your heart—just ask me.

I don't just care about the big things going on in your life, I care about the small things too. I AM never too busy to help you...so come to Me, just ask for what you need.

Lord God, thank You for always hearing my prayers.
I get tired and frustrated and I need You to help me to
have peace in my heart, knowing that You are with me.

Amen.

I'll Calm Your Fears

Praise be to the God and Father of our Lord Jesus Christ, the Father of compassion and the God of all comfort, who comforts us in all our troubles, so that we can comfort those in any trouble with the comfort we ourselves receive from God.

2 Corinthians 1:3-4 (NIV)

- o - ~~ - - o -

When you're upset, confused, or afraid, what do you do first? I always need you to come to Me before you do anything. Always pray to Me when you don't know what to do.

I can calm your fears, I can give your heart peace, and I will always give you hope when you're confused. Remember that I can do the impossible, so keep asking Me for miracles in your life.

Dear God, please calm my fears. Thank You for always being there to comfort me when I have troubles in my life and helping me when I don't know what to do.

Amen.

You're Not Forgotten

Oh LORD, how long will You forget me?

Psalm 13:1

– o – ~~ – – o –

I know that when life gets hard, it seems like I've forgotten about you, but I never forget about you. I AM always thinking of you—I love you and I care about everything in your life.

I want you to learn to be strong, knowing that I'm with you. I will always keep the promises that I have made to you. I do not lie. I want you to trust Me to always do what's best for you because I know your life from beginning to end.

Heavenly Father, thank You for never forgetting about me. Sometimes I feel so alone and like no one cares, and I need to know that You are there and You love me.

Amen.

Be Strong

The LORD Almighty is my strength.
He makes my feet like those of a deer.
He makes me walk on the mountains.

Habakkuk 3:19 (GW)

$- o - \sim\!\!\sim - - o -$

There will be many times in your life when you feel really weak, like you just can't do whatever it is you're supposed to do. And that's okay. I AM your strength when you are weak, and My power is greater than anything. I want you to need Me so I can help you to be strong.

Sometimes being strong means giving up... giving up your worries and your anger and your fears. You might be facing giants that are making you afraid, you might be looking at a big mountain in front of you that seems impossible to climb. You don't have to do it alone... pray to me and let Me help you do what you think you can't.

Heavenly Father, thank You for loving me and helping me when I am weak. Give me the strength to know that I can do anything with You and nothing is impossible.

Amen.

Get Ready

Get ready; be prepared!

Ezekiel 38:7

- o - ∿ - - o -

You don't need to worry about the problems in your life. I will help you—just believe that I will. When life gets hard, I want you to learn to come to Me for help and trust Me by getting ready for My miracles in your life.

When life is difficult, I need you to learn to focus on Me and not be afraid of whatever is going on in your life. Pray to Me, wait on Me, and get ready for My miracles.

Lord, help me not to worry, but to get ready for all the wonderful things You will do in my life.

Amen.

TIME TO REFLECT

When You Need Help...

You will ask God for what You want and need.

JAMES 4:2

You will praise God who comforts you when you're in trouble and need help, because with His comfort you can comfort others when they need it.

2 CORINTHIANS 1:3-4

You will look to God, knowing that He never forgets you and is always there to help you.

PSALM 13:1

You will rely on God as your strength.

HABAKKUK 3:19

You will get ready and be prepared for the wonderful things God has in store for your life!

EZEKIEL 38:7

What I've learned this week about needing help...

_____

_____

_____

_____

_____

_____

_____

_____

_____

_____

_____

_____

_____

_____

_____

Build Others Up

Encourage one another and build each other up.

1 Thessalonians 5:11 (NIV)

— o — ∿ — — o —

It's easy to just care about what is going on in your own life, but I will take care of everything in your life, if you will be helpful to others.

If My heart is in you, you are always looking for ways to give to others, to encourage others and to help them whenever you can. I have given you so many talents so that you can help Me to help others on earth. If you will focus on being kind and loving to others, I promise you that I will take care of you in all the ways you need Me to.

Heavenly Father, help me to open my eyes and ears for all the ways that I can help You to help others.

Amen.

Be a Blessing

Praise be to the God and Father of our Lord
Jesus Christ, who has blessed us in the heavenly
realms with every spiritual blessing in Christ.

Ephesians 1:3 (NIV)

- o - ~~ - - o -

I help you in many ways in your life so that you can help others. You might not always feel like helping others, but I will always bless you if you will be a blessing to others.

I want you to be kind and loving to those who are your friends and even to those who are not. I want others to see Me in you. Be thankful for all I've done for you and all I've given you and find ways where you can be a blessing to others.

Lord God, help me to find ways to help others so that they can see You in me. Thank You for always taking care of me.

Amen.

Give Freely

"Give as freely as you have received!"

Matthew 10:8

- o - ~~~ — - o -

Sometimes you will want what others have, but I want you to be happy with what I've given to you. I know it feels really great to "get" things, but I want you to learn to "give" more.

Pray to Me about what you need and want, and then focus on ways you can give to others. I AM always looking for ways to give to you, so that you can be a blessing to the world around you.

Heavenly Father, help me to give to others
and trust that You will always give me what
I need, so that I don't have to worry.

Amen.

Try to See Things My Way

"It is more blessed to give than to receive."

Acts 20:35 (NIV)

– o – ～～ – – o –

I want you to see others through My eyes. I want you to see all that is around you. Others need love, help, and a friend. You can spend time with those who are lonely, smile at those who are frowning and pray for those who are sick. My power works in you.

I know that learning to give to others when you need things is hard. Don't get down and discouraged—focus on what others need and how you can be a blessing and you will find more blessings in your life than you can imagine.

Lord, I want to see things the way You see them. I want to help others and focus on what makes You smile.

Amen.

Look to Me in Heaven

"I assure you *and* most solemnly say to you, unless you repent [that is, change your inner self—your old way of thinking, live changed lives] and become like children [trusting, humble, and forgiving], you will never enter the kingdom of heaven."

Matthew 18:3 (AMP)

— ○ — ∿ — — ○ —

When you are troubled and worried, where do you look? Are you looking up to Me, your Heavenly Father? When you need something, you can come to Me and trust that I will help you.

I want you to be full of faith, knowing that I will give you all that you need from day to day. Don't worry about tomorrow. I will take care of all that troubles you ... nothing is too hard for Me and I love you and will always help you.

Heavenly Father, I come to You, wanting You to help me with my faith. I pray that You will give me strength not to worry and to always trust You.

Amen.

When You Feel Selfish...

You will encourage others and lift them up.

1 THESSALONIANS 5:11

You will praise God, who has blessed you
with every spiritual blessing in Christ.

EPHESIANS 1:3

You will give as freely as you've received.

MATTHEW 10:8

You will remember to give because God has
said it is more blessed to give than to receive.

ACTS 20:35

You will repent (change, turn about)
and become like a little child [trusting,
lowly, loving, forgiving], so that you
can enter the kingdom of heaven.

MATTHEW 18:3

What I've learned this week about being selfish...

_____

_____

_____

_____

_____

_____

_____

_____

_____

_____

_____

_____

_____

_____

_____

_____

_____

Listen Carefully

You will hear a voice behind you saying,
"This is the way. Follow it,
whether it turns to the right or to the left."

Isaiah 30:21 (GW)

- o - ⌇⌇⌇ - - o -

I know that it's hard when you can't hear My voice "out loud", speaking, like you'd like to hear Me, but that doesn't mean I'm not speaking. Sometimes I speak to your spirit and your heart, sometimes I speak to you through other people in your life.

You should always be looking for Me in your life, always be listening, and know that I AM with you always. I will speak to you about big things and small things. I care about everything in your life...be still and listen for My voice.

Lord God, help me to listen for Your voice, to be still and know that You will speak to me when I pray to You.

Amen.

DAY 107

Tell You Which Way to Go

"I will instruct you and teach you in the way
you should go; I will counsel you [who are
willing to learn] with My eye upon you."

Psalm 32:8 (AMP)

There are many different ways you can live your life.
There are many choices you will have to make. The
wrong way can sometimes seem like the right way
because wrong things sometimes seem fun.

But that's why I've given you My Spirit inside you, so
that you will not be lied to, so that you will hear My
voice to help you know which way to go; because
My way is the only way that will give you peace and
happiness.

Heavenly Father, help me to follow the path that You want
for me. When I'm confused, please speak to me so that
I do not go down wrong roads which can harm me.

Amen.

Watch for Surprises

Jesus said, "Blessed rather are those who
hear the word of God and keep it!"

Luke 11:28 (ESV)

─ o ─ ∿ ─ ─ o ─

I want you to have an exciting life that's full of My
surprises. Life won't always be easy, and there will
be troubles, but I work miracles and I can turn bad
things into good things.

When you're not sure about life and things are confusing and hard, know that you don't have to have
everything figured out...you know Me and I know
everything. Just be at peace, pray to Me and watch
for My surprises.

Lord, help me to hear Your voice, to look for miracles,
and expect You to show up when I need You.

Amen.

DAY 109

Listen for the Truth

"The thief comes only in order to steal and kill and destroy. I came that they may have *and* enjoy life, and have it in abundance [to the full, till it overflows]."

John 10:10 (AMP)

Sometimes it will be really hard to tell the difference between the truth and a lie. It's easy to live your life based on how you feel. Feelings and emotions are very strong, so you must always ask what the Bible says about your situations in life.

I've given you the Bible as your instruction book for life. The Bible gives you My promises, so that you can be sure of what is the truth and what is a lie. So, when you're confused, come to Me, read My Word, the Bible, and you will know the truth.

Dear God, it's hard sometimes to know what is the truth and what is a lie, please help me to know the difference with the help of Your Spirit, so that I do not sin.

Amen.

Walk This Way

Let those who are wise understand these things. Let those with discernment listen carefully. The paths of the LORD are true and right, and righteous people live by walking in them. But in those paths sinners stumble and fall.

Hosea 14:9

– o – ⟶⟶⟶ – – o –

I know that faith is hard. It's easier to believe in what you can see instead of what you can't. Faith means that you trust in Me without seeing Me, it means you believe in the Bible and that it is My voice speaking to you, telling you which way to go, what to do, or what to say.

You won't always understand things in your life, which is why you need My help. So pray to me and keep praying. Call on Me and I will answer you.

Lord, faith is really hard sometimes. I want to believe, but sometimes I doubt. Help me to read Your Word and listen to what it says so that I will do what is right.

Amen.

TIME TO REFLECT

When You Need to Hear God...

Listen to God's voice behind you saying,
"This is the way. Follow it,
whether it turns to the right or to the left."

ISAIAH 30:21

You will turn to God who will instruct
you and teach you in the way you
should go; while He counsels you
with His eye upon you.

PSALM 32:8

You will hear the word
of God and keep it
and be blessed

LUKE 11:28

You will listen to God and follow His Word so
that you will enjoy life, and have it in abundance
(to the full, till it overflows).

JOHN 10:10

You will listen carefully to God so that
you don't sin and stumble and fall.

HOSEA 14:9

What I've learned this week about hearing God's voice...

_____

_____

_____

_____

_____

_____

_____

_____

_____

_____

_____

_____

_____

_____

_____

_____

_____

_____

I Already Know What You'll Say

"Your heavenly Father already knows."

Matthew 6:32

- o - ∿ - - o -

Sometimes you think I'm too busy for you or that I don't care about the small things in your life. But all things are small to Me—I AM God. If I can keep all the planets moving around the sun, if I keep the whole world together, I can do everything I need to keep your world together.

I know every detail of your life and I know exactly what to do to make sure that everything in your life turns out for good.

Heavenly Father, I will remember that I can pray to You about anything...big things and small. Help me to trust You to do the impossible in my life.

Amen.

Just Ask Me

If you need wisdom, ask our generous God,
and He will give it to you.
He will not rebuke you for asking.

James 1:5

- o - ∿ - - o -

When you need anything...come to Me. Whatever it is...come to Me and ask. Don't try to figure things out on your own, don't get upset because you don't understand.

I know all, I can do all, just ask Me for help and I will always do what is best for you. Trust Me when you're confused and be calm and sure that I hear you and I will help you.

Lord, I come to You asking for help because I don't understand my life sometimes. I'm asking You to help me be at peace and know that You are with me.

Amen.

Seek Me and Find Me

Search for the LORD and for His
strength; continually seek Him.

1 Chronicles 16:11

Many times your troubles get in the way of your relationship with Me. You are so upset and angry that you forget to just come to Me so that I can help you. Your worries can leave you weak and hurting, but spending time with Me will give you peace and strength.

When you play hide-and-seek, it's about finding... but I'm not hiding—I want you to seek Me and I've promised you'll find Me.

Dear God, I need You to calm my fears and give me peace
so that I am not angry with all that is wrong in my life.
Help me to seek You always and look to You for strength.

Amen.

I Will Hear You

Listen to my cry for help.
Pay attention to my prayer.

Psalm 17:1

— o — ~~ — — o —

I hear your cries for help, I know when your heart is breaking. I want you to rest and trust in Me to help you. Don't forget that I do miracles—those things that you think are impossible.

I'm full of surprises. When you pray to Me, trust that I'll take care of you and do whatever needs to be done. I love you more than you will ever know—My help is on the way.

Lord, I need Your help...I am sad, lonely, and my heart is breaking. Please love me and fill me with Your peace.

Amen.

DAY 117

Pray All the Time

Pray continually.

1 Thessalonians 5:17 (NIV)

— o — ∿∿∿ — — o —

When you don't know what to do—pray. When you're not sure what to say—pray. When you feel alone and confused—pray. I want you to pray all the time, talking to Me about everything and asking for My help over and over again.

There's nothing more important in your life than your relationship with Me and there's no one other than Me that can perform the miracles you need and all you must do is pray.

Father, thank You for being there for me. Thank You for listening to all my prayers. Please, stay with me forever.

Amen.

When You Need to Pray...

You will remember that God knows about all of your needs.

MATTHEW 6:32

You will ask God to give you wisdom.

JAMES 1:5

You will search for the Lord and for His strength and you will continually seek Him.

1 CHRONICLES 16:11

You will cry to God for help and He will listen and you will know that He is paying attention to your prayer.

PSALM 17:1

You will pray continually, all the time, without stopping.

1 THESSALONIANS 5:17

What I've learned this week about prayer...

A Battle Is Raging

The one who is in you is greater
than the one who is in the world.

1 John 4:4 (NIV)

— o — ∿∿ — — o —

Most of the time, you think your fights are just with the people and things around you—parents, friends, life that's just going badly. But there is a bigger battle. There is an enemy, the devil. And since you are Mine, he wants to destroy your life or just make you frustrated and angry.

So, first, you need to realize you are in a battle, but it's not always against the things in this world. It's a battle in the spiritual world. To fight these out-of-this-world battles, you must pray and keep praying. Let Me fight your battles for you.

Heavenly Father, I need Your help to fight my battles because I don't always know what to do and I can be easily lied to. I will keep praying to You for help so that I can win the battles in my life.

Amen.

Reject the Devil's Lies

For every child of God defeats this evil world,
and we achieve this victory through our faith.

1 John 5:4

– o – ∿∿ – – o –

Don't let all of the things going wrong in your life make you angry and upset. That will only make things worse. I know you might feel angry with Me sometimes for letting these things happen, but you should know that I've promised to take care of you through it all.

Don't believe the devil's lies. He will try to make you believe that everything is your fault or things will never get better. But you know what is truth...you know what I've promised you...just trust in what I've promised.

Lord God, please help me to trust in all that You've told me so that I don't have to be afraid of the devil and his lies.

Amen.

Think About Me

Fix your thoughts on what is true, and honorable and right, and pure, and lovely, and admirable. Think about things that are excellent and worthy of praise.

Phillipians 4:8

— o — ∿∿ — — o —

You have a lot of thoughts in your head each day. Some good, some bad, and they can make you feel really mixed up. The most important thing is to remember that I AM God.

I AM with you always, so you can't allow your thoughts and your feelings to control you. Remember that I'm in control. Don't let bad thoughts make you do bad things. Think about what you're thinking about and then remember what I've promised you— go to the Bible.

Heavenly Father, help me to think about everything that is true, pure, right and lovely. Help me think of You, Lord.

Amen.

DAY 123

Come to Me for Help

Submit yourselves, then, to God.
Resist the devil, and he will flee from you.

James 4:7 (NIV)

— o — ∿ — — o —

There is nothing for you to fear, I AM always with you. Things may not be going right in your life, but I will help you through it all. You have an enemy, the devil, but he can never defeat Me—so you must come to Me for help and trust Me to help you fight.

You don't need to run or hide—I will help you face your fears. You must learn to face your fears with your faith and trust in My power to save you.

Dear God, help me not to fear. Things in my life are hard and I am afraid of being alone. Help me to know that You are with me always and You will protect me.

Amen.

Rely on My Power

This is not a wrestling match against a human opponent. We are wrestling with rulers, authorities, the powers who govern this world of darkness, and spiritual forces that control evil in the heavenly world.

Ephesians 6:12 (GW)

— o — ∿ — — o —

I know that it's easy to believe that you are wrestling, fighting, with parents or friends, and even enemies; but there is only one enemy that you need to focus on—it's the devil that wants to trick you—he's the one you're wrestling with.

When you must fight against powers not in your world, you must fight them with My Word, Truth. Know that when you feel frustrated. You need to pray to Me so that you have all of My power to help you.

Lord God, thank You for helping me fight my battles and giving me strength to have faith that You will keep me safe against all that is evil.

Amen.

TIME TO REFLECT

When You're Struggling Inside...

You will trust in God who is greater
than the one who is in the world.

1 JOHN 4:4

You will remember that you're a child of God
and you will defeat this evil world, and will
achieve this victory through your faith.

1 JOHN 5:4

You will think of things that are true,
honorable, right, pure and lovely.

PHILIPPIANS 4:8

Your will surrender to God and not allow the devil
to mess with your life, so that he will go away.

JAMES 4:7

You are wrestling in a spiritual world.
The way to win the battle is to pray and
surrender to God who will fight your battles for you.

EPHESIANS 6:12

What I've learned this week about struggles...

I Will Mend Your Heart

He heals the brokenhearted and
bandages their wounds.

Psalm 147:3

— o — ∿ — — o —

I want you to know that I know when your heart is breaking, I know every tear you cry. I know that when you're hurting, you feel all alone, but you are never alone.

I AM always with you. I know you try to pray, but it's hard sometimes. It's when your heart is breaking that you need Me most. I can heal your broken heart— I've promised you that I will.

Heavenly Father, my heart is breaking and I need Your
love to help me not to feel so alone. Please heal me.

Amen.

I Will Refine You

When He tests me, I will come out as pure gold.

Job 23:10

— ○ — ∿ — — ○ —

I know that sometimes you feel like your troubles will never end. The problems in your life can seem to happen over and over. Know that all of your pain will someday be turned to joy.

Everything is going to be okay...even though it doesn't seem like it right now. When it seems like there is no hope, I want you to put your hope in Me and know that as bad as things seem right now, they will get better.

Lord God, even though life is hard,
help me to have hope and realize that
You are going to make everything better.

Amen.

I Will Lift You from the Pit

He lifted me out of the pit of despair, out of
the mud and the mire. He set my feet on solid
ground and steadied me as I walked along.

Psalm 40:2

Sometimes you might feel like you are in a dark hole.
You feel so alone, sad and empty and it may feel really dark. But even when you feel that way, you are
not alone and there is nothing to fear. I AM with you.

I will heal your breaking heart—just come to Me. I
know it seems like everything keeps going wrong,
but I will make sure that all things turn out for good.
Pray to Me—and I will pull you out of the pit.

Heavenly Father, when life is really hard, I feel like I'm in
a pit and I need to know that You are with me. Help me
to know that all things are going to turn out for good.

Amen.

I AM Holding You Close

Even if my father and mother abandon
me, the Lord will hold me close.

Psalm 27:10

— o — ~~~ — — o —

When you are sad and lonely, I know that you're not sure you believe in Me. I know that it's hard to believe in Me when you can't see Me. But the truth is I AM always with you, always around you—protecting you and holding you close.

I know that you have hope as to how things should turn out in your life, and when things don't go the way you want them to, it makes you upset. I want you to know that I love you and I will always help you and I AM always holding you.

Lord, hold me close and give me peace that there is hope
and I don't need to worry about the problems in my life.

Amen.

I Will Fill You

My soul thirsts for God, for the living God.

Psalm 42:2 (NIV)

– o – ∿ – – o –

When you're lonely and hurting, I know it feels like there is no one that understands or can help you. But I AM always here with you. When your heart feels empty, it's like when you're "thirsty"—you get a drink of water.

When you feel like nothing is going right and you feel all alone, I want you to thirst for Me. I can fill you up with My love, peace and joy, even when everything is a mess—I will help you to be okay... just come to Me...thirsty.

Dear God, I am lonely and hurting and I need to feel Your love and peace. I come to You thirsty.

Amen.

TIME TO REFLECT

When You Feel Broken...

You will believe that God
has promised to heal your broken
heart and bandage your wounds.

PSALM 147:3

You will trust that God
will use the bad things in your
life to make you a better person.

JOB 23:10

You will trust that God will
bring you out of the pit and set your feet
upon a rock making your footing firm.

PSALM 40:2

You will know that the Lord
is holding you close.

PSALM 27:10

You will thirst for God.

PSALM 42:2

What I've learned this week about feeling broken...

Be Careful

I don't really understand myself, for I want to do what
is right, but I don't do it. Instead, I do what I hate.

Romans 7:15

- o - ~~~ - - o -

There will always be chances to do wrong things, and sometimes wrong things can seem like good things. And that's hard. That's why I need you to stay close to Me and pray to Me constantly.

You need help when life is confusing. Just because you see others doing something, doesn't mean it's the right thing. I want you to come to Me when you're not sure what is right or wrong. Don't let anything get in the way of your relationship with Me.

Heavenly Father, thank You for always forgiving me when
I do wrong things. I want to always do what makes
You smile. Help me to do right even when it is hard.

Amen.

Ask for Forgiveness

"I tell you the truth, unless you turn from your
sins and become like little children, you will
never get into the Kingdom of Heaven."

Matthew 18:3

Everyone makes mistakes. But when you make mistakes, I want you to come to Me. I don't want you
to feel bad inside when you do wrong things. When
you come to Me and talk to Me about what has gone
wrong and what you've done, I can forgive you and
I can fill you with peace again.

So don't wait when you've done something wrong,
don't allow the bad feelings inside to make you feel
worse—come to Me for help and I will forgive all of
your mistakes.

Lord God, I mess up and it makes me feel bad inside.
Please help me to remember to come to You, so that You
can forgive me and I don't have to keep feeling guilty.

Amen.

You Will Be Forgiven If You Ask

He has removed our sins as far from us as the east is from the west. The LORD is like a father to His children, tender and compassionate to those who fear Him.

Psalm 103:12-13

— o — ∿ — — o —

When you feel bad inside from doing wrong things, and making bad choices, you want to run and even hide. Those feelings are called guilt.

Guilt makes you feel bad, but I can help you by taking the guilt away. When you come to Me and tell Me about what is making you feel guilty, I make those bad feelings go away. I use My love to forgive you and help you to know that you can let go of guilt and make better choices.

Lord, thank You for always helping me to let go of my guilt because You forgive me of the wrong things I do. I need to know that You love me even when I mess up.

Amen.

Seek My Forgiveness

"I will forgive their wickedness,
and I will never again remember their sins."

Jeremiah 31:34

$- \circ - \sim\sim - - \circ -$

I want you to always make good choices, but I know that sometimes it's hard. We all make mistakes. But, I still love you. Nothing can separate you from My love. So don't be afraid to come to Me and tell Me what you've done or why you're feeling bad inside. I already know, but I want you to learn to come to Me and talk to Me, so that I can forgive you and help you.

When you come to Me and you tell Me you are sorry for those wrong things you've done, you can know that I've forgotten it all. I will fill you with My love.

Heavenly Father, I am thankful that even though I make bad decisions sometimes, You still love me and help me to let go of my guilt and start making better choices.

Amen.

Run to Me

"Pray that you will not fall into temptation."

Luke 22:40 (NIV)

- o - ∿ - - o -

You should know that wrong choices begin with wrong thoughts. For you to have right thoughts, you need to always be praying to Me, and always reading the Bible, so you won't believe lies and make wrong choices.

I know it's hard, but you can always come to Me for forgiveness if you make a mistake. What is going on inside you is what comes out. So, I want to fix what is inside of you—I will help you.

Lord, I need Your help so that I do not sin.
Help me to keep my eyes on You and not believe
the lies that take me down wrong paths.

Amen.

TIME TO REFLECT

When You Do Wrong Things...

You will seek God to do what is right
and try not to do wrong.

ROMANS 7:15

You will turn to God and away from your sins.

MATTHEW 18:3

You will go to God and seek
His forgiveness for your sins and be
thankful for His love and compassion.

PSALM 103:12-13

You will ask God for forgiveness and praise Him for
forgetting your sins and getting rid of your guilt.

JEREMIAH 31:34

You will continually pray that God will keep
your heart pure and keep you from sinning.

LUKE 22:40

What I've learned this week about doing wrong things...

_____

_____

_____

_____

_____

_____

_____

_____

_____

_____

_____

_____

_____

_____

_____

_____

_____

_____

My Grace Is Enough

*"My grace is all you need. My power
works best in weakness."*

2 Corinthians 12:9

— o — ∿ — — o —

I know that when you do wrong things, you don't think you deserve to be loved and forgiven, but I always forgive when you come to Me. And when you come to Me, I can give you My grace—grace is My love and forgiveness even if you don't deserve it.

My grace is all you need. So don't think that just because you make a mistake that you are all alone—you are never alone...I AM always with you.

Dear God, thank You for Your love that forgives me and sets me free from all of my wrong choices. Help me to have more faith and rely on Your grace.

Amen.

I AM with You

"I am the LORD God of all humanity.
Nothing is too hard for Me."

Jeremiah 32:27 (GW)

- o - ww - - o -

Sometimes the troubles in your life might seem too big, but nothing is too big for Me—I can do anything—nothing is too hard for Me.

I want you to learn to come to Me when life is hard and you feel all alone. Always remember that I AM with you. Always know that I love you and will help you in whatever ways you need Me.

Lord, I am so thankful that You are my God and that there is nothing You can't do...I can always hope for the impossible because of Your love for me.

Amen.

DAY 143

I'll Strengthen You

It is God who arms me with strength
and keeps my way secure.

Psalm 18:32 (NIV)

— o — ∼∼∼ — — o —

When you feel alone, I know that you feel weak.
When you think there is no one to help you, it's easy
to feel like nothing is going to get better and things
will only get worse. But I AM with you to give you
hope.

I know all about your dreams, all that you wish for. I
want you to have good things in life, but sometimes
that means trusting Me in the hard times too. I will
make you stronger as you learn to come to Me and
trust Me.

Heavenly Father, thank You for giving me strength
when I am weak and feeling all alone. Help me to
be sure of the hope that You've promised to me.

Amen.

My Power Will Fill You

For the word of God is living
and active *and* full of power.

Hebrews 4:12 (AMP)

I think sometimes you forget that My power lives within you. Through your faith, when you believe in Me, I AM always with you, living in you, to help you in every way.

But you must trust in My promises, which is My Word, the Bible. My Word is alive, it has power and accomplishes all that I have promised it will. So, I want you to always trust in Me so that My power will always be inside of you.

Lord God, fill me with hope in the promises of Your
Word and help me to always trust You as my God.

Amen.

Stand Firm

Stand firm and hold fast to the
teachings we passed on to you.

2 Thessalonians 2:15 (NIV)

– o – ∿ – – o –

At times, life will be very hard. It will be really hard to tell what is truth and what is a lie, which is why I want you to always be seeking Me and making sure you are getting advice from Me.

I want you to always get your strength from Me—always pray to Me, read the Bible and listen for Me to speak to you in your heart. When life is hard and confusing, know that I AM always with you...I will always help you.

Heavenly Father, when life is hard, help me to hold on to You. I want to know You better and have stronger faith.

Amen.

When You Feel Alone...

You will trust that God's grace is all you need.
And that His power works best in your weakness.

2 CORINTHIANS 12:9

You will have hope because God is with
you and nothing is too hard for Him.

JEREMIAH 32:27

You will trust in God who arms you with strength
and keeps your way secure.

PSALM 18:32

You will remember that the Word of God is
living and powerful.

HEBREWS 4:12

You will stand firm and hold fast to the
teachings God has given you in the Bible.

2 THESSALONIANS 2:15

What I've learned this week about feeling alone...

_____

_____

_____

_____

_____

_____

_____

_____

_____

_____

_____

_____

_____

_____

_____

_____

_____

Get Up!

How long will you lie there, you sluggard?
When will you get up from your sleep?

Proverbs 6:9 (NIV)

- o - ∿∿ — - o -

Sometimes, when things aren't going well for you, you're tempted to get down and discouraged and nothing can make you happy. But sometimes, you just have to decide to "get up", to do things that you love doing, so that you aren't so sad.

Life is not always going to be easy and things won't always go the way you want them to, but I've promised to work all things together for good. Everything will be okay.

Lord God, please help me when I'm discouraged and unhappy. Fill me with peace and joy when life is hard.

Amen.

I'll Make a Way

Some men came carrying a paralyzed man on a mat and tried to take him into the house to lay him before Jesus. When they could not find a way to do this because of the crowd, they went up on the roof and lowered him on his mat through the tiles into the middle of the crowd, right in front of Jesus.

Luke 5:18-19 (NIV)

It may seem like there is no way to fix a situation or get through it. But when you're stuck, know that I will always make a way. All you must do is trust Me and not give up. Don't stop praying and hoping.

My ways may not always be easy, and you may not always be able to escape problems, but I will always be with you and make a way through it all. And along the way I will give you joy, peace, and happiness.

Heavenly Father, sometimes it seems that my problems in life are even impossible for You. Help me to trust in Your Word that nothing is impossible for You.

Amen.

Don't Look Back

Jesus told him, "Anyone who puts a hand to the plow
and then looks back is not fit for the Kingdom of God."

Luke 9:62

- o - ~~~ - - o -

I know that sometimes you get focused on the past,
what you've done right and all that's gone wrong. I
want you with Me—right now—focusing on My love
for you and not being discouraged by the problems
in your life.

I will always help you, so do not fear. Just trust Me,
do all that I ask you to do...and don't look back...
always be looking forward in faith.

Lord, help me to keep my eyes on You and to always
focus on the good things in my life, and not all
of my problems that will one day disappear.

Amen.

I Will Raise You Up

The LORD Himself goes before you and will be
with you; He will never leave you nor forsake you.
Do not be afraid; do not be discouraged.

Deuteronomy 31:8 (NIV)

—o — ∿∿ — — o —

Don't allow yourself to be discouraged and full of
fear—make sure you're focusing on the good things
in your life. Think about what is true, what is right,
what is good.

Many times your feelings get in the way of your faith
in Me and you get sad and can't seem to be happy.
When you're down and feeling all alone, remember
to pray and to trust Me to fill you with My love. I will
lift you out of the pit.

Dear God, I feel like I'm in a pit that I can't
get out of. Life is too hard and I need hope.
Please help me to know that You love me.

Amen.

Look Straight Ahead

Look straight ahead, and fix
your eyes on what lies before you.

Proverbs 4:25

— ○ — 〜〜 — — ○ —

There will be a lot of disappointments in your life. Sometimes life is hard because of things you do, sometimes it's just because things go wrong. But whatever is causing you to be down, if it's something you've done, your wrongs can be made right, and I will use all the bad things in your life for good.

I just want you to keep your eyes on Me and keep believing. When life is too hard for you, it's never too hard for Me—just trust Me and look straight ahead to all of the good things I have in store for you.

Lord God, help me to look forward to the hope that You give me. It's so easy for me to look at how hard life is, instead of all of the blessings You have promised to me.

Amen.

TIME TO REFLECT

When You're Discouraged...

You will get up and be filled
with hope because God is good.

PROVERBS 6:9

You'll remember that God always makes a way.

LUKE 5:18-19

You will keep focused on the blessings God
has in store for you and not lose hope.

LUKE 9:62

You will remember that you should not
be afraid because God is with you.

DEUTERONOMY 31:8

You will look to God and His blessings
and know that He is with you and
you need to keep focused upon Him.

PROVERBS 4:25

What I've learned this week about being discouraged...

Be Patient

O LORD, how long will You forget me?

Psalm 13:1

– o – ∿∿ – – o –

When you pray, I know that sometimes it can seem like I don't hear you or My answers are taking too long. I know that you think you need things "right now", but sometimes waiting is better.

There's no reason for you to be sad or discouraged when My miracles don't happen right away—I want you to trust Me, even when it seems like nothing is going to happen. That's what faith is and true faith keeps believing no matter how long it takes.

Lord, I feel like You've forgotten me and it doesn't seem like You are going to answer my prayers. Please give me patience, Father.

Amen.

Trust in Me

Commit everything you do to the Lord.
Trust Him, and He will help you.

Psalm 37:5

- o - ~~~ - - o -

While you're waiting on your prayers to be answered, I want you to have faith, while you're waiting. I know it's hard to believe that your prayers will be answered, when you can't see things changing.

But while you're waiting, I want you to be thankful, to be looking for ways to help others and be kind. Waiting in faith doesn't mean doing nothing.

Heavenly Father, while I wait on Your answers to my prayers, help me to do the things You want me to as I wait.

Amen.

Remember My Perfect Timing

"At the right time, I, the LORD, will make it happen."

Isaiah 60:22

- o - ∿ - - o -

When you have to wait on Me, you learn how much faith you do or don't have. Sometimes I use your "waiting" times to teach you to trust Me more, and not to give up.

So don't always think that just because you don't see Me answering your prayers right away that the miracles you're praying for aren't going to happen. Faith in Me keeps trusting, even if things get worse before they get better. Trust that My miracles will come at just the right time.

Lord God, help me to have faith to trust that You will answer my prayers when You think it is the best time.

Amen.

Stay Thankful

Because of our faith, Christ has brought us into this place of undeserved privilege where we now stand, and we confidently and joyfully look forward to sharing God's glory.

Romans 5:2

– o – ∿ – – o –

When you're waiting, I want you to enjoy each and every day. I don't want you waiting and being sad and discouraged. I want you to live each day with joy and happiness, knowing that I will answer your prayers.

I've given you each day to be happy and know that even when things are really hard, everything is going to be okay. Keep looking up to Me, keep praying, and keep being thankful, each and every day.

Heavenly Father, help me to have joy,
even as I wait on You to answer my prayers.
Fill me with hope and gratitude.

Amen.

See How Much You Need Me

As the deer pants for streams of water,
so my soul pants for You, my God.

Psalm 42:1 (NIV)

— o — ∿ — — o —

You may not realize it, but waiting on Me will help you to see how much you need Me. When you need Me, it draws you closer to Me and makes our relationship stronger.

So when you have to wait, it may seem hard and like you are waiting for nothing, but if you will use those times of waiting to seek Me more, you will not waste time waiting. Waiting for Me is needing Me and you'll learn that you can always count on My miracles.

Lord, I truly need You and I feel like hope is gone. Please have mercy on my heart and fill my soul with Your Spirit.

Amen.

TIME TO REFLECT

When You're Waiting...

You will remember that the Lord has
promised never to forget you.

PSALM 13:1

You'll commit everything you do to the Lord.
You will trust Him, and He will help you.

PSALM 37:5

You will trust that God
has promised you that,
"At the right time, I,
the Lord, will make it happen."

ISAIAH 60:22

You will be grateful, confident and joyfully look
forward to sharing God's glory.

ROMANS 5:2

As the deer pants for streams of water,
you will pant for your God.

PSALM 42:1

What I've learned this week about waiting...

_____

_____

_____

_____

_____

_____

_____

_____

_____

_____

_____

_____

_____

_____

I AM with You

We must continue to hold firmly to our declaration
of faith. The one who made the promise is faithful.

Hebrews 10:23 (GW)

- o - ~~ - - o -

When things don't happen when you think they
should or how you think they should, I know it's hard
to trust that I AM still with you. But if I've made a
promise to you, I will keep it.

There is never a reason for you to worry or be afraid.
I want you to be sure that I AM with you and that I
will answer your prayers. So when it seems like you
are on your own because nothing is happening in
your life, trust Me more and hold on to your faith.

Heavenly Father, help me to hold on to my faith
when I'm doubting and having a hard time in life.

Amen.

I Will Never Fail You

Not one word has failed of all the wonderful
promises He gave through His servant Moses.

1 Kings 8:56

- o - ∿∿ — - o -

You get worried that I won't help you, that I won't
keep My promises. I know it's because life is hard and
sometimes when you pray, you're not sure I'm listening, but I promise, I AM.

I've made you promises and I do not lie. You should
always know that I will keep My promises even if you
do wrong things, or even if you doubt My power. I
will still keep My promises. So, know that no matter
what, I will never fail you.

Father, sometimes I wonder if You can help me. My
problems seem so big that they are all I see. Help me
remember that You are greater than any problem, and
You'll help me with them. Because You keep Your promises.

Amen.

You Are Safe in My Arms

The eternal God is your refuge,
and underneath are the everlasting arms.

Deuteronomy 33:27 (NIV)

– o – ∿ – – o –

You don't need to see Me or feel My presence to know that I'm with you and holding you. When you are afraid, I want you to pray right away. I want to strengthen you and fill you with hope so you will know that everything is going to be okay.

Even though you don't always see what I AM doing, you can trust that I AM with you...I will help you and I'm holding you.

Dear God, I need to know that You are holding on to me because I feel so alone and afraid when life is hard.

Amen.

I Hear Your Prayers

With Him is only the arm of flesh, but with us is the
Lord our God to help us and to fight our battles.

2 Chronicles 32:8 (NIV)

— o — ∿ — — o —

Many days it can seem like you're in a battle. Things
in life aren't going right, and no matter what you do,
it seems to be wrong.

No matter what, you need to keep praying—that's
how battles are won—on your knees, praying. I AM
with you throughout it all.

Lord, I need Your help because I feel like I'm always in
a battle and I get tired of fighting. Help me to rest
and know that You will help me fight these battles.

Amen.

I AM Faithful

No temptation has overtaken you except what is common to mankind. And God is faithful; He will not let you be tempted beyond what you can bear. But when you are tempted, He will also provide a way out so that you can endure it.

1 Corinthians 10:13 (NIV)

You are always going to be tempted to do wrong things. The devil wants you to believe that lying, cheating, and doing things to get what you want now, is what is right for you. But doing wrong things, making decisions without Me, never lead to good things.

So, don't be fooled into thinking that if something makes you feel good that it is good for you. Sometimes things will make you feel good, but it's bad for you—it's against what I've told you to do. Just keep close to Me, pray to Me when you're confused, and be full of faith.

Heavenly Father, thank You for always helping me to do right things and forgiving me when I don't.

Amen.

TIME TO REFLECT

When You Need God's Promises

You will continue to hold firmly to your declaration of faith. Knowing that the one who made the promise is faithful.

HEBREWS 10:23

You will remember that God has not failed one word of all His good promises.

1 KINGS 8:56

You will trust that the eternal God is your refuge, and He holds you in His everlasting arms.

DEUTERONOMY 33:27

You will remember that the Lord your God will help you to fight your battles.

2 CHRONICLES 32:8

You will trust that God is faithful. He will not let you be tempted beyond what you can bear. He will always provide a way out to do the right thing.

1 CORINTHIANS 10:13

What I've learned this week about and trusting God's promises...

_____

_____

_____

_____

_____

_____

_____

_____

_____

_____

_____

_____

_____

_____

_____

_____

_____

_____

Stay at My Feet

Exalt the LORD our God and worship
at His footstool; He is holy.

Psalm 99:5 (NIV)

- o - ~~~ -- o -

When you worship Me, praising Me for who I AM—
your God—your Savior—I see your faith. If you to-
tally trust Me, if you focus on Me instead of your
problems, you'll find yourself at My feet.

I want you to let go of trying to be in control of your
life. Only I can do what you can't—only I can do the
impossible. And it's when you're focused on Me,
praising and worshiping Me, that miracles happen.

Lord, I am so thankful for who You are...for Your love and
Your forgiveness, for Your grace that always saves me.

Amen.

Know That Nothing Is Too Hard for Me

"O Sovereign LORD! You made the heavens and earth by Your strong hand and powerful arm. Nothing is too hard for You!"

Jeremiah 32:17

- o - ~~ -- o -

I know that sometimes you're worried that your troubles are too hard and I can't answer your prayers, but you need to know that NOTHING is too hard for Me.

I want you to see Me as being bigger than all of the problems in your life. And then I want you to trust Me to do what is best. Know that I will never fail you and then trust that I can do the miracles you need Me to.

Lord God, help me to know that You can do anything and nothing is too difficult or impossible for You, even when things seem hopeless.

Amen.

DAY 171

There Is Power in Praise

> Paul and Silas were praying and singing hymns
> of praise to God. Suddenly, a violent earthquake
> shook the foundations of the jail. All the doors flew
> open, and all the prisoners' chains came loose.
>
> Acts 16:25-26 (GW)

When you feel like things are bad and just getting worse, when the only thing that can change things is a miracle, know that I will help you and there is power in your praise.

When you praise Me and thank Me for all I've done and all I'm yet to do, know that I hear your faith and My power will be released from heaven. And even when life is hard, I want you to praise Me, it shows what you expect Me to do—to help you, to save you, to give you hope.

Heavenly Father, help me to praise You, expecting Your power in my life. Give me hope when I have none.

Amen.

Sing Prayers of Praise

It is good to give thanks to the LORD,
to sing praises to the Most High.

Psalm 92:1

— o — ⌇⌇⌇ — — o —

When you pray to Me, I want you to pray to Me full of praise and filled with hope. You may not feel like there is anything in your life to be praising Me for, but you can't see and know all that I do.

I AM in control of all that concerns you. Even though you can't always see what I'm doing, I AM always at work, always making all things work together for good. There is nothing for you to fear. Just give thanks and pray with praise.

Lord God, I pray to You full of praises. My heart is filled with hope because my hope is in You and I know that You have promised to turn all things together for good.

Amen.

The Time Is Now

"The time is coming—indeed it's here now—when true worshipers will worship the Father in spirit and in truth. The Father is looking for those who will worship Him that way."

John 4:23

There may never seem to be a right time to pray, but every moment of your life you should be praying and when you come to Me in prayer, I want you to be full of hope and praise.

I want you to come into My presence, ready to hear My voice as I speak to your heart. I want you to trust Me...that even though nothing seems to be going right, I AM working to keep My promises to you. So, call on Me, believe in Me, the time to pray and hope is right now.

God, help me praise You every second of every day in prayer. Open my heart and let me hear Your voice.

Amen.

TIME TO REFLECT

When You Need to Praise God...

You will bow down and
pray to God because He is Holy.

PSALM 99:51

You will praise God who
made the heavens and
earth by His strong hand
and powerful arm and remember
that nothing is too hard for God!

JEREMIAH 32:17

You will remember that
God does things suddenly.

ACTS 16:25-26

You will give thanks to God
and sing praises to Him.

PSALM 92:1

Here and now you will worship
God and praise Him for all He is,
all He has done and all He is yet to do.

JOHN 4:23

What I've learned this week about praising God...

_____

_____

_____

_____

_____

_____

_____

_____

_____

_____

_____

_____

_____

_____

_____

Know My Love Is Perfect

God showed His great love for us by sending
Christ to die for us while we were still sinners.

Romans 5:8

─ o ─ ∿ ─ ─ o ─

You cannot imagine how much I love you. And I know sometimes, because life is so hard, you wonder if I even love you at all. My love for you never fails and it never ends. Even when you make mistakes, I still love you.

You can always come to Me and I will forgive you. Jesus died on the cross to save you, so that your sins can be forgiven and you don't have to feel guilty. That's what My love does for you and there is no greater love.

Heavenly Father, thank You for loving me no matter what mistakes I make. I need to know that I can always come to You for help.

Amen.

You're Saved by Grace

Because of His great love for us, God who is rich in mercy, made us alive with Christ even when we were dead in transgressions—it is by grace you have been saved.

Ephesians 2:4-5 (NIV)

- o - ∿ - - o -

I know that you feel like you're always having to work so hard to do right things and you just feel like life is too difficult and you just can't do it. And often times, because of your mistakes, you feel like you don't deserve to be loved.

But that's what grace is for. Grace means I give you My love and forgiveness, even if you don't think you deserve it. So come to Me when you need love...I will always love you—no matter what.

Lord God, thank You for Your grace that saves me. Thank You that I can have peace that You love me no matter what. Amen.

Be Flooded with Light

I pray that your hearts will be flooded with light
so that you can understand the confident hope
He has given to those He called—His holy people
who are His rich and glorious inheritance.

Ephesians 1:18

— o — ∿∿ — — o —

When you're weak, I can make you strong. I AM with you always to help you step-by-step with whatever you need help with in life. You can always come to Me when you are feeling down or afraid and when life's problems make things seem dark and gloomy.

My love can flood the darkness with light. I AM all you need, you just need to come to Me, praying, and expecting Me to help you.

Dear God, sometimes I feel really weak and I lose hope. Please help me to remember that I don't have a reason to be sad because You will fix everything.

Amen.

DAY 179

You Already Have It

Even if my father and mother abandon
me, the LORD will hold me close.

Psalm 27:10

– o – ∿ – – o –

Sometimes you will feel unloved. You may not feel loved by family or even friends—but you are always loved by Me. Even when you make mistakes, even when you've really done wrong things, you can always come to Me and I will love you.

So even though it might seem like others have abandoned you, and it feels like no one cares, you can be sure that I never stop loving you and I AM always holding you close.

Lord God, sometimes I feel unloved and I need to know that You still love me. I don't like it when I do wrong things, but I make mistakes and I am thankful that I can come to You.
Amen.

Give Your Whole Heart

Seek the LORD your God with all your heart and soul.

1 Chronicles 22:19

- o - ~~~ - - o -

I love you more than you will ever know. You were created to know Me, to walk with Me through this life, and to look forward to spending eternity with Me.

You will never fully understand how much I love you and all of the amazing plans I have for your life. I AM all you need to experience the peace and joy you're supposed to have in life. But I need you to completely trust Me. Keep seeking Me with all of your heart and soul.

Heavenly Father, help me to understand how much You love me, so that I can have peace and joy even when life is hard.
Amen.

TIME TO REFLECT

When You Need God's Love...

You will remember that even though you do wrong things, God still loves you.

ROMANS 5:8

You will be thankful for God's mercy and His grace that has saved you.

EPHESIANS 2:4-5

You will know that God has given you hope because He loves you no matter what.

EPHESIANS 1:18

You will trust God to always hold on to you.

PSALM 27:10

You will seek the Lord God with all your heart and soul.

1 CHRONICLES 22:19

What I've learned this week about needing God's love...

_____

_____

_____

_____

_____

_____

_____

_____

_____

_____

_____

_____

_____

_____

_____

_____

_____

_____

Choose Peace

Make every effort to live in peace...
and to be holy; without holiness
no one will see the Lord.

Hebrews 12:14 (NIV)

– o – ~~~ – – o –

There will be so many things in life that make you feel afraid, worried, or disappointed. All of these things try to steal your peace and make you feel like things are bad and will never get better.

But if you are hoping in Me, you can have My peace all of the time. My peace doesn't care what is going on in life, My peace is the same no matter what... and you can have My peace if you keep trusting Me, even when you're not sure you can.

Lord God, thank You for Your peace that
helps me to be calm even when life is not.

Amen.

You'll Find Rest with Me

The LORD gives strength to His people;
the LORD blesses His people with peace.

Psalm 29:11 (NIV)

— o — ∿ — — o —

When you're frustrated and tired of life, when you are worried and afraid, it is trusting in Me that will give you the peace you need to rest. I want you to learn to rely on Me and rest, even when there are lots of troubles in life.

Every time something goes wrong in life, you should use that time to remind yourself to come to Me, to trust in Me, so that I can help you more. If you will come to Me, I will always give you all the grace, peace, and strength you need.

Heavenly Father, I get frustrated and tired and want to give up. Please help me to rely on You and Your strength, so that I can be calm and peaceful when life is hard.

Amen.

Know My Perfect Peace

"You will keep in perfect *and* constant peace *the one* whose mind is steadfast [that is, committed and focused on You— in both inclination and character], Because he trusts *and* takes refuge in You [with hope and confident expectation]."

Isaiah 26:3 (AMP)

Things in your life might change, but I do not change. I AM the same yesterday, today, and forever. I know that sometimes you get frustrated with your life and you feel like all you do is cry because of your sadness, but know that I AM with you through it all, I catch every tear.

Even when life is hard, even when things don't get better, you need to trust Me and be filled with hope and peace. Know that even though you might feel alone, you are not. I AM always with you and working on all that is important in your life.

Lord, please give me Your peace. I feel restless and I am having a hard time calming down because of how crazy life feels.

Amen.

Find Peace in Believing

I pray that God, the source of hope, will fill you completely with joy and peace because you trust in Him. Then you will overflow with confident hope through the power of the Holy Spirit.

Romans 15:13

— o — ∿ — — o —

Life can get difficult in a hurry and it's hard to make good decisions when your feelings are messed up with anger, sadness or fear.

So, know that if you're having a hard time believing, I will strengthen you and give you peace to keep having faith and to believe in Me to help you with everything in your life. I just need you to keep believing and I will fill you with hope and joy and give you peace in believing.

Heavenly Father, I need Your peace because my feelings keep me from thinking straight and hearing Your voice. Strengthen me and help me to believe.

Amen.

Seek Me

Seek peace and pursue it.

Psalm 34:14 (AMP)

— ○ — ∿ — — ○ —

You need to have My peace so that you can have peace with others. And in order to have My peace, you have to seek it, because it will be hard to find peace when things in life aren't going right and when things seem unfair.

But you should always know that you can have My peace if you will pray to Me. I will always help you with whatever you need Me to and I will always give you strength and peace when you are tired and weak. All you need to do is seek Me.

Lord, help me to seek Your peace and to be calm even when life is hard and unfair. Help me to focus on You and not on my problems.

Amen.

TIME TO REFLECT

When You're Restless...

You will make every effort to live in peace...
and to be holy.

HEBREWS 12:14

You will ask God to bless you with
His peace and strengthen you.

PSALM 29:11

You will ask God to guard you and keep you in
perfect and constant peace as you keep your
mind focused on Him. You will commit yourself to
Him, lean on Him, and hope confidently in Him.

ISAIAH 26:3

You will be filled with joy and peace because you
are trusting in God and you're overflowing with
confident hope given to you by the Holy Spirit.

ROMANS 15:13

You will search for God's peace
and work and keep His peace.

PSALM 34:14

What I've learned this week about feeling restless...

_____

_____

_____

_____

_____

_____

_____

_____

_____

_____

_____

_____

_____

Stay on the Level Path

Teach me Your way, O LORD,
And lead me on a level path.

Psalm 27:11 (AMP)

− o − ∿ − − o −

I know that believing in Me is not easy. When you can't see Me, when you have troubles in life and you don't feel like I'm answering your prayers, it's easy to lose your faith in Me. But don't allow yourself to question who I AM and why I do things the way I do.

You must trust that I have made promises to you and I will keep them. Keep trusting Me, even when you're confused because there are so many lies that can take you down paths that are not good for you. Pray to Me and I will teach you and lead you on My perfect path for your life.

Heavenly Father, teach me to always look to You when I'm confused and to trust Your Word to lead and guide me.

Amen.

Know Whom to Trust

Some trust in chariots and some in horses,
but we trust in the name of the LORD our God.

Psalm 20:7 (NIV)

— ○ — ∿ — — ○ —

Each and every day you have to decide whom you are going to trust. Sometimes you think you can trust your friends, but then they let you down and you don't feel you can trust anyone. But you can trust Me. I never lie and I always keep My promises. When you put your trust in Me, you will never be disappointed.

You won't always understand what I'm doing and I might not do things exactly the way you want Me to or when you want Me to, but you can be sure I will always do what is best for you.

Lord, when life gets hard it is really difficult for me to believe. Help me to always look to You right away and trust in all that You've promised, keeping my eyes on You.
Amen.

Believe Without Seeing

We fix our eyes not on what is seen,
but on what is unseen.

2 Corinthians 4:18 (NIV)

– o – ∿∿∿ – – o –

When life is really hard, I know it seems impossible to believe in something you can't see. But I want to grow your faith and help you learn that if you believe...you will see. I want you to learn to have faith in Me at all times—trusting Me for all your needs.

There is never anything for you to fear, I AM with you always and I'm always looking over you and protecting you. When life gets confusing, keep praying to Me and keep your eyes on Me—and...just believe.

Dear God, help me to believe so that I will
see Your promises come true in my life.

Amen.

Have Faith

it is impossible to please God without faith. Anyone who wants to come to Him must believe that God exists and that He rewards those who sincerely seek Him.

Hebrews 11:6

- o - ~~ — - o -

I need you to trust Me. When you trust in Me, it shows Me your faith and your faith in Me makes everything possible and miracles will happen in your life.

When you are afraid, you're not trusting in Me. When you are having troubles, you need to go to My promises in the Bible and know that I never lie, and I always keep My promises. You can trust Me with your past, present, and future—I will take care of you and I will always help you—but nothing happens without faith.

Lord, sometimes I'm afraid. Please give me Your peace so that I can rest and be calm, knowing that You will always take care of me.

Amen.

Don't Doubt

"I tell you, you can pray for anything,
And if you believe that you've received it,
it will be yours."

Mark 11:24

- o - ~~ - - o -

I want you to be sure that I hear your prayers. When you pray, you show Me that you have faith in Me. I want you to learn to pray big prayers and little prayers. Tell me all about what is important to you and ask Me for even the little things.

I don't want you to doubt, I want you to learn to always believe. Although life can be hard, I want you to know that faith is simple. Every time life gets difficult, you have the opportunity to believe—to have a little faith.

Heavenly Father, help me to have simple faith...to just believe what You've promised and not question or doubt.

Amen.

TIME TO REFLECT

When You Battle to Believe...

You will ask God to teach you His ways
and lead you in a straight path.

PSALM 27:11

You will choose to keep trusting in God
and nothing or no one else.

PSALM 20:7

You will believe what
God has promised you,
you will keep believing
no matter how things look.

2 CORINTHIANS 4:18

You will continue to believe
that God exists and that He will bless
you if you continue to seek Him.

HEBREWS 11:6

You will pray and believe that God
will answer your prayers.

MARK 11:24

What I've learned this week about believing in God...

_____

_____

_____

_____

_____

_____

_____

_____

_____

_____

_____

_____

_____

_____

_____

_____

I Can Do All Things

Put your trust in the LORD.

Psalm 4:5 (ESV)

- o - ~~~ - - o -

Life is hard, but you are not alone. I know it's easy to feel alone, but you are never alone, I have promised to be with you always. It might seem like there is no hope, but hope is never gone, if you're trusting in Me.

When you think that I'm not hearing your prayers, when I seem far away and silent, know that I'm wanting you to seek Me more and learn to trust Me in bigger ways. And remember: There is nothing I can't do.

Lord God, thank You for never leaving me alone and always helping me to have faith when life is hard.

Amen.

Believe with All Your Heart

"Do not be afraid. Stand firm and you will see
the deliverance the LORD will bring you today."

Exodus 14:13 (NIV)

– o – ∿∿ – – o –

There's something you should know—I can do any-thing. I have all the power. You don't need to be afraid, I AM always with you. It might seem like you're all alone, or like no one cares, but there is no one that cares more than I do and no one loves you like I do.

Don't get all upset about all of the problems in your life. Sometimes I allow bad things because they lead to good things. And sometimes the hard things just give you the chance to believe in Me more.

Lord, I am thankful that You are always
with me to help me fight my battles.
Help me to not be afraid and to just believe.

Amen.

Know Everything Is Possible in Me

"Everything is possible with God."

Mark 10:27

— o — ∿ — — o —

I see you where you are, but I also see where you are going. You might feel stuck, like the things in your life are just too hard, but nothing is too hard for Me and everything is possible when you're trusting in Me.

Don't lose hope when things seem impossible. Don't be afraid when things don't seem to be going right. Remember that I AM always in control and you can put your hope in Me, I can do anything and everything.

Dear God, sometimes I feel stuck and I need to know that You will help me. Fill me with hope so that I can rest knowing that You can do anything.

Amen.

Get Up Again

"Get up! For the Lord has given you victory."

Judges 7:15

- o - ᨠᨠ - - o -

I know you sometimes feel sad and like there is no hope or help for the problems in your life, but I AM your hope and I AM always with you to help you.

Sometimes you will just need to make the decision to believe in Me and choose to hope even when it seems like nothing is going right and things aren't changing. There are times when you are just going to have to get up and choose to believe and choose to have joy because you know that I AM with you.

Lord, help me to be sure of what I believe and to know that I can trust You to help me and I can have hope.

Amen.

DAY 201

Grow Strong

No unbelief made Abraham waver concerning
the promise of God, but he grew strong in
his faith as he gave glory to God.

Romans 4:20 (ESV)

– o – ∿∿ – – o –

I want you to grow strong in your faith and sometimes that will mean that you must go through hard
things. It's the same as how your muscles grow, by
using them more and more.

So, instead of seeing troubles in life as bad things,
see them as ways to grow in your faith. Look at hard
times as opportunities to believe in Me more and a
chance to see miracles. So, don't try to always figure
things out, all you need to do is keep looking to Me
and trusting Me and your faith will grow stronger.

Heavenly Father, I want to be strong in my faith even when
I have to go through hard things. Help me to see the hard
times in my life as a chance to grow closer to You.

Amen.

TIME TO REFLECT

When You Feel Life Is Hard...

You will put your trust in God.

PSALM 4:5

You will not be afraid and you will
look for God to save you.

EXODUS 14:13

You will remember the promise in the Bible
that says, "Everything is possible with God."

MARK 10:27

You will not stay stuck in your sadness
or loneliness. God will save you and
give you victory over your battles.

JUDGES 7:15

You will refuse to doubt, no matter what.
You will grow strong in your faith by
believing what God has promised.

ROMANS 4:20

What I've learned
this week about hard times in life...

_____

_____

_____

_____

_____

_____

_____

_____

_____

_____

_____

_____

_____

_____

My Joy Will Make You Strong

Don't be dejected and sad, for the
joy of the LORD is your strength!

Nehemiah 8:10

— o — ⁓ — — o —

I always want you to be filled with peace and joy, but I know that it is not always going to happen. When life is hard and things aren't going the way you want them to, I know you get frustrated and angry. It's okay to feel that way, but I don't want you getting stuck in your feelings.

I give you hope...there is no reason to stay stuck in feeling empty and sad. When you feel weak and you start to doubt, pray to Me and I will strengthen you and give you joy.

Lord, help me not to be sad just
because life is hard. Fill me with Your joy
so that I can enjoy the life You've given me.

Amen.

Keep On Praying

Rejoice in our confident hope. Be patient
in trouble, and keep on praying.

Romans 12:12

— o — ⌇⌇⌇ — — o —

Sometimes there may not be a lot to be joyful about. Sad things happen in life, and those things can make you sad and even angry. But the joy I give to you is much different than just a feeling.

I want you to learn that your joy comes from believing in Me, believing that I can do the impossible and trusting Me to do what is best for your life. And believing means that you keep praying and wait patiently for me to take care of everything in your life.

Heavenly Father, help me to have hope and be
patient as I wait on You to answer my prayers.

Amen.

Always Be Joyful

Always be joyful.

1 Thessalonians 5:16

- o - ~~~ -- o -

It won't be easy to always be joyful. There are things in life that can leave you feeling empty, angry, and afraid. That is why I always want you trust in Me and staying close to Me, by praying to Me, so that when life gets hard, I can give you My strength and My joy.

Your joy will come from praying to Me and asking for My help. I will give you the hope you need to keep believing in Me and the power I have to work miracles in your life. I want you to understand that I AM the reason for your joy.

Lord, help me to be full of joy even when I'm dealing with hard things in my life. Help me to know that You are my joy.

Amen.

Great Things Are Ahead

The LORD has done great things
for us, and we are filled with joy.

Psalm 126:3 (NIV)

— o — ∿ — — o —

You don't need to worry about the future, you just need to trust that I love you and will always do what is best for you. Know that I have great things in store for you.

I see your life from beginning to end and I know all of the things that will grow your faith and make you happy. So just pray and keep believing in the hope I give you. Don't be worried, don't be afraid, and know that I can and will do great things.

Lord, help me to count my blessings and know that even though things might seem bad, You have great things in store for my life.

Amen.

Receive Blessings from Above

Blessed are the people to whom such blessings fall!
Blessed are the people whose God is the LORD!

Psalm 144:15 (ESV)

— o — ∿ — — o —

You may not realize it, but My blessings fall on you like rain. I AM always looking for ways that I can bless you. I AM always looking over your life and everything that is important to you. I hear every prayer and I want to give you your heart's desires.

I may not always give you everything you want because everything you want may not be what is best for you. So, you must trust Me and know that I will always give you what is the very best for you.

Lord, I know that I do not always see the blessings
You give to me. Thank You for always giving me
what I need and loving me no matter what.

Amen.

TIME TO REFLECT

When You're Feeling Down...

You will not doubt
and you will keep believing
in God's promises to you
while you praise Him.

NEHEMIAH 8:10

You will rejoice in hope,
be patient when there is trouble,
and you will keep on praying.

ROMANS 12:12

You will always be joyful.

1 THESSALONIANS 5:16

You will be filled with joy because the Lord
has done great things for you.

PSALM 126:3

You will remember that you are
blessed because God is your Lord.

PSALM 144:15

What I've learned
this week about feeling down...

_____

_____

_____

_____

_____

_____

_____

_____

_____

_____

_____

_____

_____

_____

_____

_____

_____

I'm Always Here for You

Give thanks to the LORD, for He is good!
His faithful love endures forever.

1 Chronicles 16:34

– o – ∿ – – o –

My love for you is not just love...it is also mercy. Mercy is what My love gives. Even when you make mistakes and do wrong things, I forgive you and love you.

Even when you have messed up and you haven't made things right, you should come to Me, so that I can help you. I can help you not to feel so bad about yourself, just because you have made a mistake. I can help you know how to fix the mistakes you've made so you can make better choices. I AM always here for you.

Lord, even though I mess up, I am so thankful that You
are loving and forgiving and You have mercy on me.

Amen.

I Will Give You Mercy

Your mercy toward me is great.
You have rescued me from the depths of hell.

Psalm 86:13 (GW)

– o – ∿∿ – – o –

Each and every day you will need My mercy. You will never be perfect, and you will always make mistakes. So, every morning, I give you My mercy to start your day.

I want you to pray to Me all through your day. I want you to always ask for help. No matter how difficult things are—there is nothing I can't do. I will use My mercy to lead you to blessings, all you have to do is trust in My love for you. I have great mercy for you each and every minute.

Heavenly Father, thank You for Your mercy that helps me each and every day to know that You love me.

Amen.

Pray When You Wake Up

I will sing of Your strength, in the morning
I will sing of Your love; for You are my fortress,
my refuge in times of trouble.

Psalm 59:16 (NIV)

— o — ∿ — — o —

I want you to start praying to Me before you even get out of bed. Don't wait to ask for My help after the day has started and you find yourself with lots of problems. Seek Me, My help, and My mercy is ready for you first thing, in the morning.

If you will seek Me, first thing in the morning, My mercy will give you courage, strength, wisdom, patience and peace.

Dear God, I come to You asking for help. I need You to always lead and guide me, to help me make the best decisions.

Amen.

Be Thankful for My Perfect Gifts

Every good present and every perfect gift comes from above, from the Father who made the sun, moon, and stars. The Father doesn't change like the shifting shadows produced by the sun and the moon.

James 1:17 (GW)

I AM only good. You should always expect good and perfect gifts from Me. I always want to bless you. I want you to always have hope in My promises, so that you can have peace and so that you will have faith and not doubt.

Every day you will have to decide to receive all the blessings that I want to give you. Trust Me to know what is best for you. And when I don't do what you think I should, when I should, trust My timing.

Lord, thank You for all of the amazing blessings You give to me even though I don't deserve them all.

Amen.

Count Your Blessings

For You are God, O Sovereign Lord. Your words are truth, and You have promised these good things to Your servant.

2 Samuel 7:28

— o — ∿ — — o —

I have promised you good things. You need to remember that when things aren't going well, and you're scared and worried, I have promised you more blessings than you can count.

As you pray to Me, My Spirit will remind you of the promises I've made to you. I do not want you to miss out on the blessings I have for you because you forget to pray to Me and you don't ask for My blessings. Be still and know that I AM God and I will bless you.

Heavenly Father, thank You for the promises of good things. Help me to be still and know that I can always trust You for all I need.

Amen.

When You Feel Like Life is Falling Apart...

You will give thanks to the Lord, for He is good! His faithful love endures forever.

1 CHRONICLES 16:34

You will remember that God's mercy toward you is great. He has rescued you from the depths of hell.

PSALM 86:13

You will sing of God's strength, in the morning you will sing of His love; for He is your fortress, your refuge in times of trouble.

PSALM 59:16

You will trust that every good present and every perfect gift comes from above, from the Father who made the sun, moon, and stars. The Father doesn't change like the shifting shadows produced by the sun and the moon.

JAMES 1:17

You will remember that God is God and He is sovereign. You will remember all that God has promised to you.

2 SAMUEL 7:28

What I've learned this week about when it feels like my life is falling apart ...

_____

_____

_____

_____

_____

_____

_____

_____

_____

_____

_____

_____

_____

_____

_____

Don't Worry, Be Happy

"Can all your worries add a single moment to your life?"

Matthew 6:27

 — o — ∿ — — o —

I know that when your life is hard, it is easy to worry. But try not to focus on your problems. I need you to focus on Me and all of the promises I've made you.

You will find that there will always be problems in life that will make you want to worry. Your worries don't mean anything when you have My promises. I don't want you wasting your time worrying. Let Me handle all of your problems—trust Me to do miracles.

Lord God, help me not to worry, but to trust that You have everything under control and You only have good things planned for my life.

Amen.

Believe in My Goodness

I believe that I will see the goodness of
the LORD in this world of the living.

Psalm 27:13 (GW)

- o - ~~ - - o -

I want to bless you more than anything you can hope
for or imagine. You can believe in My goodness. I
have promised you that I will work all things together
for good.

I know it's not always easy to believe in Me and all
that I've promised you—especially when things seem
to get worse and not better. I AM working in your life,
you will find that sometimes things might look bad,
but I AM using them for good. Believe it, and you will
see.

Heavenly Father, thank You for Your goodness,
for Your love and kindness and the promises
You've made to me to give me hope.

Amen.

Have Unshakable Faith

Declare me innocent, O Lord, for I have acted with integrity; I have trusted in the Lord without wavering.

Psalm 26:1

– o – ∿∿ – – o –

Everything that happens in your life, the big things and the small things, will require My help. Constantly pray to Me, so that your faith will be unshakable.

You won't always be able to control what is going on in your life, but you can completely trust Me to always be in control...to love you, to help you, to protect you, to give you hope. I want you to always have faith and joy. Know that I AM with you always.

Lord God, help me to trust that You are God all the time, not just sometimes. Fill me with faith so that I will not fear.

Amen.

Just Remember ...

But then I recall all You have done, O LORD; I remember Your wonderful deeds of long ago. They are constantly in my thoughts. I cannot stop thinking about Your mighty works.

Psalm 77:11-12

It won't always be easy to keep believing and having hope when things don't seem to be getting better. So, you will need to be constantly seeking Me and paying attention to My Word, the Bible.

You cannot decide to believe only when things are going your way, you must always believe. And if you have a hard time, just remember the ways I have helped you in the past and how I've answered your prayers before—know that I will continue to bless you.

Dear God, I remember all of the little prayers You've answered and all of the big ones. Help me to have faith even when it's hard to believe sometimes.

Amen.

Live By Faith

"My righteous ones will live by faith.
But I will take no pleasure in anyone who turns away."

Hebrews 10:38

— o — ⌇⌇⌇ — — o —

You need to have faith for My power to work in your life. Truly believe in the promises I've made to you. That's where My power is.

Don't rely on your feelings and emotions to decide whether or not you believe because feelings and emotions can trick you. That is why you should always pray to Me right away, so that I can lead and guide you with My Spirit. There's no reason to be worried or afraid—all you need is faith.

Heavenly Father, thank You for the strength
You give me to keep believing even when I'm
feeling doubtful. Help me not to worry.

Amen.

TIME TO REFLECT

When You Doubt...

You will not worry because it
takes away your joy in life

MATTHEW 6:27

You will be full of faith and
believe that you will see
the goodness of the Lord
in this world of the living.

PSALM 27:13

You will continue to
trust God and not let doubt
get in the way of your faith.

PSALM 26:1

You will remember the wonderful
things God has done and you will
keep thinking about good things.

PSALM 77:11-12

I will continue to have faith
and always turn to God.

HEBREWS 10:38

What I've learned
this week about being
filled with doubts...

Don't Give Up

Don't lose your confidence. It will bring you a great reward. You need endurance so that after you have done what God wants you to do, you can receive what He has promised.

Hebrews 10:35-36 (GW)

- o - ∿ – - o -

I want you to remember to never give up. Don't lose hope just because things aren't going the way you want them to. I know what it's hard to keep hoping when bad things keep happening. But if you'll stay focused on Me, I will remind you of all the reasons to keep believing—the biggest reason is that I AM God and I can do anything.

Just because you have trouble in your life, does not mean that I've left your side. Just keep waiting for Me and expecting Me to show up—just don't give up.

Lord, help me not to lose hope, but to know that
You can do anything and I should not give up.

Amen.

Keep Hoping

As for me, I look to the LORD for help. I wait confidently for God to save me, and my God will certainly hear me.

Micah 7:7

- o - ∿ — - o -

You might feel helpless, like there is nothing you can do to fix the problems in your life, but that doesn't mean you should stop believing because it seems like there is no hope.

The things I allow in your life, the plans I have for you won't always make sense to you. Don't try to figure everything out. I want you to learn to trust Me no matter what—when things are good and when things are bad. Just keep hoping in Me.

Heavenly Father, sometimes I feel helpless and alone. I need to know that everything is going to be okay and that You are with me always.

Amen.

Nothing Can Separate You From Me

Nothing can ever separate us from God's love.

Romans 8:38

- o - ∿∿ - - o -

I know that sometimes life can get really scary. There will be times when you feel that all hope is gone and you are just a victim to all of the bad things in the world. But you are Mine and I will always protect you and take care of you.

There is absolutely nothing that can touch you without My permission. If I allow tough things in your life, I have promised that they are for reasons that I will use for good, in the end. So, trust Me and do not fear. I AM with you always.

Heavenly Father, help me not to fear anything in my life, but to constantly look to You for my peace and strength.

Amen.

I Will Give You Peace of Mind and Heart

"I am leaving you with a gift—peace of mind and heart. And the peace I give is a gift the world cannot give. So don't be troubled or afraid."

John 14:27

– o – ∿∿ – – o –

When you are afraid, come to Me right away. Do not waste time and energy worrying and being afraid. I AM in control of all things.

When you are losing hope, when you're not sure if everything is going to be okay, it's My Spirit that will fill you with unimaginable peace. You might still be going through tough times, but I will be with you and I will comfort you and give you strength to continue to believe.

Lord God, thank You for the gift of Your peace in the middle of all my troubles. I am grateful for all of Your gifts.

Amen.

Be Worry-free

Worry weighs a person down.

Proverbs 12:25

Life is hard enough without having to worry too. I know that you think that there is nothing you can do when you have trouble in your life, but you can do something...the best thing...pray.

Pray to Me about everything that is bothering you... everything that is making you afraid and worried. I can give you peace, I can speak to your heart and calm you. I can give you My grace so that you can rest knowing that I will take care of you and all of your troubles. Don't become more afraid by worrying, focus on My promises to you...I will work all things together for good.

Dear God, help me not to worry so much, but to focus on Your promises and be at peace knowing that You have everything under control.

Amen.

TIME TO REFLECT

When You're Anxious...

You will keep your faith and be strong, knowing that God will always fulfill His promises to you.

HEBREWS 10:35-36

You will look to God for help. You will wait confidently for God to save you because you know that God hears your prayers.

MICAH 7:7

You will remember that NOTHING can take you away from God and that He is always with you protecting you.

ROMANS 8:38-39

You will not be troubled or afraid because God gives you His peace.

JOHN 14:27

You will refuse to worry and only pray.

PROVERBS 12:25

What I've learned this week about being anxious...

_____

_____

_____

_____

_____

_____

_____

_____

_____

_____

_____

_____

_____

_____

_____

Renew Your Heart

I desire to do Your will, my God;
Your law is within my heart.

Psalm 40:8 (NIV)

- o - ~~ — - o -

There will be a lot of things in life that you do not understand, but if you trust Me, I will fill your heart with everything that is in My Word, the Bible, and you won't get frustrated trying to understand. You will just trust Me to be in control and to do what is best.

Your faith in Me puts a new heart in you, filled with My Spirit. I will help you to always want to do what is right and when you make mistakes, you will quickly come to Me to ask for forgiveness.

Heavenly Father, help me to do what is right
and to trust Your Word to lead and guide me.

Amen.

DAY 233

Remember, My Plans Are for Good

Whatever happens, conduct yourselves in
a manner worthy of the gospel of Christ.

Philippians 1:27 (NIV)

– o – ∿ – – o –

Feelings can make things seem like they are out of control, when they're really not. You won't always understand life and that can be confusing. But when you have faith in Me, you can know that I AM in control and there is nothing for you to fear—I AM always in control and My plans for you are always good.

Trusting in Me gives you peace in your heart, even when life is really hard and you're feeling alone, sad, scared, and confused. Come to Me and I will always help, love and protect you no matter what happens.

Lord, my feelings make me feel out of control
and I need You to fill me with Your peace so that
I can have faith no matter what happens.

Amen.

Don't Worry
You're Not God

We rely on what Christ Jesus has done for us.
We put no confidence in human effort.

Philippians 3:3

- o - ∿∿ - - o -

I know that it's easy to try and take control of your own life and feel like you can do it on your own, but you can't. Have hope in Me and be confident that I will always take care of you.

When you have troubles in your life, I want you to come to Me first, and know that I will help you. I want you to come to Me and tell Me that you're confused. I want you to trust that I will give you wisdom and help you to know what you should do. Simply trust in Me as your God.

Dear God, help me to remember that You are God and I'm not. I get confused and afraid and sometimes I try to take over. Please help me to trust You to take care of my life.

Amen.

Pay Attention

Let those who are wise understand these things. Let those with discernment listen carefully. The paths of the LORD are true and right, and righteous people live by walking in them. But in those paths sinners stumble and fall.

Hosea 14:9

— o — ⌇⌇⌇ — — o —

Things are not always what they seem to be—life can be confusing and tricky. At times your feelings will make you feel like things are really bad, and they're not. When you're confused and frustrated and not sure about what to do, you need to pay close attention to Me, so that I can help you.

Learning to listen to Me and hear My voice takes practice. You must pray and find time where you can sit silently. Your life doesn't always have to be so noisy. My will for your life, My desires for you are for you to always have joy, hope, and peace.

Heavenly Father, help me to always look to You and pay attention to what You have taught me through the Bible.

Amen.

I Will Guide You

All the believers were one in heart and mind.

Acts 4:32 (NIV)

— o — ∿ — — o —

I know that life pulls you in a lot of different directions, but I AM always here to help you to make sure you stay on My perfect path for you. Your heart and mind are Mine because you choose to believe in Me.

It's so easy to get sidetracked, but your faith means you're on My path, the believer's path. When you have faith in Me, I give you My heart and My mind… you have nothing to fear! Don't allow your heart and mind to be divided—you are one with Me, your God—the One who saves you.

Lord, I get confused in life and I lose my way. Help me to come to You when I'm afraid and confused so that You can guide me and give me hope.

Amen.

TIME TO REFLECT

When You Don't Understand...

You will do God's will...what is right
and wrong is in your heart.

PSALM 40:8

You will always try to do what is right and focus
on what God wants you to do.

PHILIPPIANS 1:27

You will rely on what God has done and
can do for you. You will trust Him alone.

PHILIPPIANS 3:3

You will trust that God's way is the right
way. You will follow His plan for your
life so that you will be blessed.

HOSEA 14:9

You will remember that you
have the heart and mind
of God guiding you.

ACTS 4:32

What I've learned
this week about not
understanding certain things...

_____

_____

_____

_____

_____

_____

_____

_____

_____

_____

_____

_____

_____

_____

_____

_____

Smile Even through Your Tears

God's approval is revealed in this Good News. This approval begins and ends with faith as Scripture says, "The person who has God's approval will live by faith."

Romans 1:17 (GW)

— o — ∿ — — o —

No matter what is going on in your life, no matter how hard and confusing life is, don't give up on faith. When you're full of doubt, and fear, draw near to Me in prayer and trust that I hear you and will help you.

Faith—trusting in Me—allows you to enjoy your life, even when life is really hard. When you're not sure what to do, pray to Me and trust Me to help you and do what is best, which might mean you don't always get what you pray for. Trust Me for the impossible, and be at peace, knowing that I AM with you always.

Heavenly Father, help me not to think about my feelings, but think about the hope You give me through Your promises.
Amen.

Wait and Trust

The LORD is good to those who wait for Him,
to anyone who seeks help from Him.

Lamentations 3:25 (GW)

- o - ∿∿ - - o -

When you're confused about the future, when you are afraid of what is going on in your life, don't try to understand things, realize that you won't always understand. Just come to Me, pray to Me, and I will give you strength and peace in your heart.

The answers to your prayers won't always happen right away, so many times you will have to wait. And I know waiting is hard. But when you're waiting, you can grow closer to Me and learn to trust Me more. Your faith will grow stronger when you're waiting and trusting.

Lord God, I get confused and then I get afraid, help me
to know that You are with me to help me and that even
though I have to wait, You will still answer my prayers.

Amen.

Ask Me First

"When they call on Me, I will answer;
I will be with them in trouble.
I will rescue and honor them."

Psalm 91:15

— o — ∿ — — o —

One thing you can be sure of, I AM always with you. It might not always seem like it, but you can always trust Me to help you. Call on Me, pray to Me when you're in trouble and I will save you.

If you try to understand everything on your own, if you try to make decisions without asking for My help, you will only end up with more trouble. So don't make decisions without asking Me to lead and guide you.

Dear God, sometimes it seems like You're not there. Help me to keep believing and keep praying to You, knowing that You will answer.

Amen.

Stay Close to Me

But as for me, it is good to be near God. I have made the
Sovereign LORD my refuge; I will tell of all Your deeds.

Psalm 73:28 (NIV)

- o - ∿∿ — - o -

I know that you often doubt whether I'm real and if I
really care about you. But I want you to always come
to Me when you're feeling unsure about your faith.

I know sometimes you feel angry and upset with Me
because things aren't going your way and life is just
too hard. But I want you to learn to trust Me and
realize that there is no reason to doubt or fear. Just
draw near to Me, pray to Me, and I will give you
peace and strength.

Lord, I need to know that You are with me always.
Please give me hope and strength as I trust in You.

Amen.

Focus on
My Promises

Our faith gives us sufficient courage to freely
and openly approach God through Christ.

Ephesians 3:12 (AMP)

– o – ~~~ – – o –

Don't allow yourself to give up on faith. Just because you don't see things happening when you think they should be or how you think they should be, doesn't mean something isn't happening. I dare you to believe.

I have amazing things ahead for you, but you must have faith first. I want you to keep focusing on the promises I've made you in the Bible. If you're angry and upset with Me, let me know. I can help you by giving you peace, so that you can keep believing.

Heavenly Father, help me to trust that You have
good things ahead for me even when things may not
seem good right now. Help me to keep believing.

Amen.

When You Want to Give Up...

You will continue to have faith
and believe in God's promises.

ROMANS 1:17

Even though life is hard, you will wait for God
to help you and you will trust Him.

LAMENTATIONS 3:25

You will trust that when you're in trouble
you can call on God and He will answer you.

PSALM 91:15

You will draw near to God and pray to Him so that
you will find the strength you need not to give up.

PSALM 73:28

You will go to God immediately
because He loves you and gives you
grace so that you can receive
His blessings of strength and courage.

EPHESIANS 3:12

What I've learned this week about not giving up...

_____

_____

_____

_____

_____

_____

_____

_____

_____

_____

_____

_____

_____

_____

My Grace Is Free

By grace you have been saved through faith.
And this is not your own doing; it is the gift of God.

Ephesians 2:8 (ESV)

- o - ∿∿ – - o -

Because I love you, I've given you hope through My grace, and it's free! There's nothing you can do to earn my grace or lose it. So don't get down when life doesn't go right, or you get in trouble, I will always help you when you come to Me.

So, don't think that you have to do everything right. Even when you make mistakes, I will forgive you. Just know that no matter what, I love you and nothing can take away My love for you.

Lord God, thank You for Your grace, so that even when I get in trouble, I can come to You without fear and know that You will love me and help me.

Amen.

Accept the Grace I Give

He said, "My grace is all you need. My power
works best in weakness." So now I am glad
to boast about my weaknesses, so that the
power of Christ can work through me.

2 Corinthians 12:9

Sometimes you think you need lots of things, but actually you just need Me and the grace I give you. Know that when life is really hard, I'm giving you the chance to get closer to Me, to count on Me, to learn to trust Me.

It's a way that you can grow stronger in your faith and realize that you really can trust Me. All you really need is Me—it's My grace and love that will get you through any situation. Just keep believing and trusting.

Heavenly Father, I am so thankful for Your grace
because I mess up and I need to be forgiven. Thank you
for Your love that will get me through anything.

Amen.

I AM in Control

Those who trust in the LORD will lack no good thing.

Psalm 34:10

- ○ - 〜〜 - - ○ -

I never want you to worry. I know sometimes it's hard, but you really don't need to worry because I'm always in control. There is nothing I can't do and My love for you never changes.

I want you to be sure, because I've promised you that I will always take care of you. Even if it seems like things aren't going right, you can be sure that I AM working to make all things in your life work out well.

Lord God, thank You for all of the good things in my life. I know they come from You and Your love for me.

Amen.

DAY 249

I Will Still Your Fear

Do not be anxious about anything.

Philippians 4:6 (NIV)

I want you to be sure that you can trust Me. I've made you promises and I do not lie. I know everything, and I have all the power. I watch over you—day and night—when you're awake and when you're sleeping. There is nothing at all for you to fear. You do not have to worry when you're trusting in Me.

So, when you feel like life is falling apart, know that if you trust Me, I will take care of everything. Seek Me first and you'll have all that you need.

Heavenly Father, sometimes I feel like things are falling apart and I need to know that You keep Your promises and I'll have all I need. Please guide me.

Amen.

Remember, You're Never Alone

It is not that we think we are qualified to do anything
on our own. Our qualification comes from God.

2 Corinthians 3:5

– o – ∿∿ – – o –

You need to know that I will always be with you and
I will always take care of everything that is important
in your life. There will always be hard times, there
will always be things that just don't go right, but you
can trust Me to work it all out.

I just want you to learn to be strong, to have faith
and keep believing—no matter what. I can work miracles, so you should never give up. There is nothing
that is too hard for Me.

Lord, help me to be strong and have faith and realize
that I cannot do everything on my own...I need You.

Amen.

TIME TO REFLECT

When You Need God in a Big Way...

You will be thankful for God's gift of grace to you, knowing that you cannot do anything to gain or lose God's love for you.

EPHESIANS 2:8

You will trust in God's grace when you are weak and you will look to Jesus to give you strength.

2 CORINTHIANS 12:9

You will trust in God and know that He will give you every good thing.

PSALM 34:10

You will not worry about anything. You will trust God for everything.

PHILIPPIANS 4:6

You will look to God for help because you can't do anything on your own.

2 CORINTHIANS 3:5

What I've learned this week about needing God...

_____

_____

_____

_____

_____

_____

_____

_____

_____

_____

_____

_____

_____

_____

_____

_____

_____

_____

DAY 253

I Am Always with You

Yet, I am always with You. You hold on to my
right hand. With Your advice You guide me,
and in the end You will take me to glory.

Psalm 73:23-24 (GW)

- o - ∿ - - o -

You might not know where your life is headed. Things might seem confusing, but I know your life from beginning to end and I know every decision you need to make to go down the right path.

When life is hard and confusing, you need to know that I AM always with you, so that you don't have to be afraid. Just like if we were walking in the park, I AM holding your hand, walking through life.

Heavenly Father, I find peace in knowing that You are in
control of my life and that You love me. Help me to do
what is right, so that I can live a life of blessings.

Amen.

Walk with Me

We can make our plans, but the LORD determines our steps.

Proverbs 16:9

– o – ~~~ – – o –

I know that you like to make plans for your life, you have ideas of what you want to be and what you want to do, but I want you to know that My plans for your life are way bigger and better.

So, I don't want you to try and live each day on your own. I want you to always pray to Me so that I can help you make right decisions that will lead you down the right path that I have planned for you. I'll guide you...step by step.

Lord, I look to You to lead and guide me step by step so that I will follow Your good plan for my life.

Amen.

Follow My Path

He renews my strength.
He guides me along right paths,
bringing honor to His name.

Psalm 23:3

- o - ∿ - - o -

Sometimes life will be very confusing and it will be hard to know which way to go. But remember I AM always with you. I will always help you to see which way is the right way—sometimes My Spirit will speak to your heart and you will just know what to do. Other times, you will need to read the Bible and listen for My voice in your heart.

I know the ways I lead you might not always be easy, but they are the right ways—they are My ways.

Dear God, help me to be strong even when the way You lead me in life might be hard. Help me to praise You as I walk with You.

Amen.

Trust in My Plans

"I know the plans I have for you..."

Jeremiah 29:11

- o - ~~ - - o -

When your day doesn't go as planned, try not to stop believing or praying to Me. When your life seems out of control, you need to know it's still in My control.

Even though sometimes My plans might seem too hard or like they're not leading you in the right direction, I want you to be sure that My plans are always what is best for you. And even though things might be tough, I AM with you to help you. And in the end, everything is going to work out—you don't need to worry.

Lord, help me to trust You when I'm confused and want to go my own way in life. Help me to trust in Your plans and know that You love me and will always do what is best for me.

Amen.

Trust Me to Figure It Out

The LORD directs our steps, so why try to
understand everything along the way?

Proverbs 20:24

– o – ∿∿∿ – – o –

I don't want you to always try to understand
everything in your life—because you won't. I have
amazing plans for your life, and they are for good,
but you won't always understand.

I want you to learn to let go, to be at peace, and
know that I will always strengthen you to have the
faith you need to keep trusting Me to help you with
each step of your life. Trust Me to do the impossible
and know that I will always do what is best for you.

Heavenly Father, help me to let go and let You handle all
of the detail of my life so that I don't have to worry.

Amen.

TIME TO REFLECT

When You Don't Know Which Way to Go...

You will find strength and comfort knowing that God is always with you, holding your hand and guiding you.

PSALM 73:23-24

You will trust God and His plan for your life.

PROVERBS 16:9

You will find your strength from God as He leads you down the right path.

PSALM 23:3

You will have peace knowing that God has a good plan for your life.

JEREMIAH 29:11

You won't try to understand everything in your life, but believe in God's promises for you.

PROVERBS 20:24

What I've learned this week about not knowing which way to go...

_____

_____

_____

_____

_____

_____

_____

_____

_____

_____

_____

_____

_____

_____

_____

_____

_____

Turn to Me

"If you forgive those who sin against you,
your heavenly Father will forgive you."

Matthew 6:14

— o — ⌁ — — o —

I know it's not easy to forgive others, especially when your feelings get hurt. But you have to remember that you make mistakes and you need forgiveness, too. So, I need your heart to be forgiving, just like My heart is forgiving towards you.

You need to know that forgiving means that the person who has hurt you may not say, "I'm sorry." You need to let your hurt go anyway and know that I will heal your hurting heart.

Lord, help me to forgive others, even when they
really hurt my heart. I want to have peace
and love in my heart all of the time.

Amen.

You Are Forgiven

Should we keep on sinning so that God can show
us more and more of His wonderful grace?

Romans 6:1

— o — ∿ — — o —

Just because I love you and forgive you, doesn't
mean you should do wrong things. It just means
that when you do make mistakes, you don't have to
live with the bad feelings inside that make you feel
guilty. You can come to Me and I will forgive you.

I want you to stay connected to Me, so that I can
help you make better decisions, but if you do make
mistakes, know that you can come to Me and be
forgiven, so that you can have peace and joy again.

Lord God, help me to do right things. I sometimes
make mistakes and I need to know that You
forgive me so that I can have peace.

Amen.

Remember, Others Need It Too

Jesus said, "Father, forgive them,
for they know not what they do."

Luke 23:34 (ESV)

- o - ∿∿ – - o -

Sometimes others will hurt you on purpose. Sometimes they don't really mean to hurt you. Either way, I want you to forgive them by letting go of your anger and wanting to hurt them back.

When you keep holding onto your anger, it makes your life sad and I want you to be happy. So, don't keep being angry—come to Me, pray to Me, and I will help you to forgive.

Dear God, sometimes I feel really hurt and I want
to hurt others back. Help me to let my anger go
and to let You handle the hurt in my life.

Amen.

Learn to Forgive

Be kind and compassionate to one another, forgiving
each other, just as in Christ God forgave you.

Ephesians 4:32 (NIV)

— o — ∿ — — o —

There will always be times when you get angry because of how others treat you. Sometimes they will
say sorry, sometimes they won't. But I need you to
forgive anyway.

You have My heart in you and My heart is kind and
loving. So, I want you to be kind and loving to others, even when they are not kind and loving to you. I
want you to be good to those who are evil because
it makes your heart better.

Lord, I get angry when I get hurt and when others don't
say sorry it makes me really upset. Please fill my heart
with Your love so that I can have peace and live with joy.
Amen.

I Will Fill You with Peace

"To you who are willing to listen, I say, love your enemies! Do good to those who hate you. Bless those who curse you. Pray for those who hurt you."

Luke 6:27-28

- o - ∿∿ — - o -

One of the hardest things you'll have to do is forgive someone. Others can be hurtful, even when they don't mean to be. And sometimes they will not even realize they hurt you. But all you need is My love in your heart.

I don't want you to be angry all of the time and hold a grudge. I want you to always have peace. I want you to love those who hate you and pray for those who hurt you and I will bless you.

Heavenly Father, help me to let go of my anger when others hurt me. Please fill me with Your peace and help me to love those who hurt me and are mean to me.

Amen.

TIME TO REFLECT

When You Need Forgiveness...

You will forgive others
because God forgives you.

MATTHEW 6:14

You will be thankful for
God's grace that forgives you
when you make mistakes
and stop doing wrong things.

ROMANS 6:1

You will be thankful for Jesus dying on the Cross
so that you can be forgiven.

LUKE 23:34

You will be kind to others, forgiving them,
just as in Christ God forgave you.

EPHESIANS 4:32

You will love your enemies and do good to
those who hate you. You will bless those who
curse you and pray for those who hurt you.

LUKE 6:27-28

What I've learned this week about forgiveness...

Change Your Thoughts

For as he thinks in his heart, so is he.

Proverbs 23:7 (AMP)

$- o - \sim\!\!\sim - - o -$

I know that when life isn't going just right, it's easy to just think about the bad things instead of all of the good things in your life. You have to constantly think about what you're thinking about—because your mind can get filled with bad things really fast.

So when your mind wanders, when you're confused and thinking negative thoughts, remember to pray and ask for My help to get your mind thinking things that are good.

Lord, sometimes my mind gets stuck thinking bad thoughts, help me to focus on You and think things that are good.

Amen.

Give Thanks for What You Have

I am not saying this because I am in need, for I have learned to be content whatever the circumstances. I know what it is to be in need, and I know what it is to have plenty.

Philippians 4:11-12 (NIV)

− o − ∾∾ − − o −

I know that there are lots of things you want or need, and I will always take care of you, but you have to learn to be happy with what you have before I give you more.

So when things are good, you can be really glad. When things are bad, pray and know that I will make sure that you have all you need.

Heavenly Father, I am so thankful for all that You give me in life. Help me to always praise You whether I have a little or a lot.

Amen.

I Will Bless You

The fear of the LORD leads to life, and whoever has
it rests satisfied; he will not be visited by harm.

Proverbs 19:23 (ESV)

– o – ∿∿ – – o –

I know it's hard not to want more and more in life, but I need you to learn to be happy with what you have. Sometimes I bless you with things. Sometimes I will just bless you with peace and joy.

But there is no reason for you to worry, I will always take care of you. I will always make sure that you have enough faith to keep believing that I have everything under control and everything is going to be okay.

Lord God, I worry a lot because things in life go wrong
and I'm scared that things are not going to turn out right.
Please help me to simply trust You and Your love for me.

Amen.

Stay Focused on Me

Those who seek the LORD lack no good thing.

Psalm 34:10 (ESV)

– o – ∿ – – o –

I know you worry about a lot of things in life, but I want you to let Me worry about all of the things in your life. I just want you to stay focused on Me, and enjoy your life.

You might not know all of My plans for your life, but you can be sure that they are for your good. So, enjoy your life, be happy, and know that there is nothing good that I will not give to you.

Heavenly Father, help me not to worry so much and to just stay focused on You. Help me to enjoy my life and be happy.
Amen.

Be Happy with What You Have

A heart at peace gives life to the body,
but envy rots the bones.

Proverbs 14:30 (NIV)

– o – ⁓ – – o –

I know it's hard not to want things, but I want you to learn to be happy with what you've been given because being thankful will give you a happy heart.

When you always want what others have and what you don't have, it makes your heart feel bad and takes away your joy. I want you to know that I will give you special things that others don't have. I will give you what you need and others what they need. So be thankful and you'll be happy.

Lord, help me to be happy with what I
have and to have a thankful heart.

Amen.

TIME TO REFLECT

When You Want More...

You will think about all the wonderful gifts
God has given you and be thankful.

PROVERBS 23:7

You will be happy with what you have,
no matter how much or how little that is.

PHILIPPIANS 4:11-12

You will be thankful for all that God
provides you and be at peace knowing
He will always take care of you.

PROVERBS 19:23

You will always seek God
and know that you will lack
no good thing because
He takes care of you.

PSALM 34:10

You will ask God to fill your heart
with peace and be thankful for all
of His blessings in your life.

PROVERBS 14:30

What I've learned this week about wanting more...

_____

_____

_____

_____

_____

_____

_____

_____

_____

_____

_____

_____

_____

_____

_____

_____

_____

Pray All the Time

Pray in the Spirit at all times and on every occasion.
Stay alert and be persistent in your prayers
for all believers everywhere.

Ephesians 6:18

- o - ∿∿ - - o -

I want you to pray all of the time. Not just when you need something. Praying brings you closer to Me and it keeps you from worrying so much.

Anywhere you are, at any time, you can pray. So whatever is bothering you, whatever is making you sad, I want you to talk to Me about it so you don't stay sad. I want you to let Me handle everything that makes you worry, so that you can have fun and enjoy your life.

Heavenly Father, help me to pray all of the time
and come to You when I am confused and afraid.

Amen.

Give Your Worries to Me

Turn your burdens over to the LORD, and He will take care of you. He will never let the righteous person stumble.

Psalm 55:22 (GW)

─ ○ ─ ∿ ─ ─ ○ ─

Sometimes you can get stuck thinking about all of the things that are wrong. You keep feeling upset and can't seem to feel happy or have fun. I want you to learn to give up all of those bad things and let Me handle them.

I want you to always know that you can trust Me with whatever is bothering you. I will help you with everything that is making you worried. Let Me help you.

Lord, help me to give You all of my worries.
I want to let go of my problems so that I
can enjoy the life You've given me.

Amen.

Stop Thinking "What If"

Get ready; be prepared.

Ezekiel 38:7 (NIV)

- o - ∼∼∼ - - o -

There's no reason for you to be worried or afraid when you have troubles in your life. Everything is going to be okay because I'm in control and I can do anything.

Don't let yourself keep thinking "what if". "What ifs" will only keep your mind from believing in Me.

When you have bad, worried thoughts, stop and pray to Me so that I can give your mind peace. Then you can get ready for all of the good things I have planned.

Dear God, help me to stay focused on You and look forward to the great plans You have for my life. Help me to not think about "what ifs".

Amen.

Take a Deep Breath

Praise be to the Lord, to God our Savior,
who daily bears our burdens.

Psalm 68:19 (NIV)

- o - ∿ - - o -

Your burdens, those things that you worry about, those problems that keep you from going to sleep at night, are things I should be dealing with.

So, I want you to take a deep breath and give me all of the things that are bothering you. I want you to enjoy your life and have hope because of the promises I've made you.

Lord, sometimes I can't sleep at night because I am
so worried about the problems in my life. Help me to
remember that You can handle anything and everything.

Amen.

I Will Give You Hope

"Then you will know that I am the LORD your
God who has freed you from your oppression."

Exodus 6:7

— o — ∿ — — o —

I don't want you to lose hope because of all of your worries. Your mind will play tricks on you and make you feel like things are worse than they are.

When you are feeling afraid of the future and what is going to happen, I want you to look up and pray to Me...knowing that I will help you. I can bring you out of your sadness and fill you with joy and peace. No matter what is happening in your life, just come to Me.

Heavenly Father, I feel like there is no hope when life gets really hard. My mind keeps telling me that nothing is going to get better. Please fill my heart with hope.

Amen.

TIME TO REFLECT

When You're Feeling Overwhelmed...

You will continually pray and not give up.

EPHESIANS 6:18

You will give all of your worries to God and trust that He will take care of you.

PSALM 5:22

You will focus on God's promises for you and get ready for all the good things He has planned for your life.

EZEKIEL 38:7

You will thank God for always helping you with your problems.

PSALM 68:19

You will look to God who promises to help you with your worries and take care of all of your problems.

EXODUS 6:7

What I've learned this week about feeling overwhelmed...

Know That I Will Help You

Wait for the LORD; be strong and
take heart and wait for the LORD.

Psalm 27:14 (NIV)

- o - ∿∿ — - o -

There will be lots of times in life when you feel "stuck", but I will always help you get "unstuck".

I know it's really hard when you pray and nothing seems to happen. But I want you to remember all of the promises I've made you and that I always keep My promises.

When your prayers are not answered right away, I want you to keep praying and just wait...sometimes amazing things are about to happen.

Lord God, help me to be strong and wait for You, knowing that when I pray to You, You will always answer me.
Amen.

Wait Quietly for Me

I wait quietly before God, for my victory comes from Him.

Psalm 62:1

– o – ～～ – – o –

When you're worrying, you're not fully trusting in Me. I want you to pray and be sure that I will answer your prayers. I always hear you and I will always help you.

Don't try to make things happen on your own. I AM the One who knows everything and can make the best plans for your life. So, don't worry so much, just enjoy your life and know that I will rescue you, take care of you and give you all you need...but wait quietly. Don't worry...things are going to change.

Dear God, help me to wait patiently for You to answer my prayers. Help me not to worry and just trust You.

Amen.

Look to Me for Help

We do not know what to do, but we are
looking to You for help.

2 Chronicles 20:12

- o - ~~~ -- o -

Sometimes, when you are having a hard time in life,
you need to realize that you can't always fix things.
You need Me and you need My help.

I know that things seem hopeless, like nothing is
going to change and everything is getting worse
instead of better, but I can do anything. I can do
miracles. And I like to surprise you. So, keep asking
for My help and keep looking for My surprises.

Lord, I need You and I need Your help. I sometimes
feel like there is no hope. Fill me with faith
to keep praying and keep looking to You.

Amen.

Trust Me to
Answer Your Prayers

My times are in Your hands;
deliver me from the hands of my enemies,
from those who pursue me.

Psalm 31:15 (NIV)

– o – ⌇ – – o –

I don't want you to try so hard to figure things out. The way that I do things can be confusing because I see things differently than you do. I'm God and you're not.

That's why I've given you the Bible, My promises, so that you can have hope and trust Me to do what I promise to do, when I promise to do it. My timing for answering your prayers is perfect, so just trust Me.

Heavenly Father, help me to trust that Your timing for answering my prayers is perfect and that You know what is best for me.

Amen.

Keep Hoping

We wait [expectantly] for the LORD; He is our help and our shield. For in Him our heart rejoices, because we trust [lean on, rely on, and are confident] in His holy name.

Psalm 33:20-21 (AMP)

- o - ∿ - - o -

When you're stuck, it might seem like there is no hope. But there is always hope if you're praying to Me and looking to Me for help.

I will always take care of you, but sometimes I will allow you to go through tough times so that you can learn that you need Me. You aren't meant to live your life without Me and without My help. So, when you're stuck, don't lose hope. Look to Me and I will save you.

Lord, when life gets hard and nothing is changing, I feel stuck. Please help me to remember that You will always help me and I can count on You.

Amen.

TIME TO REFLECT

When You Feel Stuck...

You will be strong and wait
for God to help you.

PSALM 27:14

You will wait patiently for God
and know that He will help you.

PSALM 62:1

When you don't know
what to do, you will look to
God for help and keep praying.

2 CHRONICLES 20:12

You will trust that God
is taking care of you at
all times and in all ways.

PSALM 31:15

You will remember that God is
your helper and He protects you.

PSALM 33:20-21

What I've learned this week about feeling stuck...

_____

_____

_____

_____

_____

_____

_____

_____

_____

_____

_____

_____

_____

_____

_____

_____

_____

I Will Strengthen Your Faith

With Christ as my witness, I speak with utter truthfulness. My conscience and the Holy Spirit confirm it.

Romans 9:1

— o — ⁓ — — o —

You can't have faith without My Spirit to help you. And you can't believe without knowing My promises that are in the Bible. So, when you're feeling empty, you must pray.

Praying tells Me you want My help, you want My Spirit to give you hope and strength. Your faith can only be real if My Spirit is in you, helping you, encouraging you, reminding you to think about what is true, about what I've promised you.

Heavenly Father, I need Your help with
my faith because sometimes I doubt.
I need Your strength and encouragement.

Amen.

DAY 289

My Spirit Will Guide You

The Spirit God gave us does not make us timid,
but gives us power, love and self-discipline.

2 Timothy 1:7 (NIV)

— o — ∿ — — o —

You should know that fear does not come from Me, it comes from the devil. So, when you're feeling afraid, pray right away and ask that you would be filled with My Spirit.

I know life can be difficult and full of negative things, but I AM always with you, and My Spirit will fill your mind with thoughts that are good and full of hope. When you are trusting in My promises for you, you will always be strong in your faith and My Spirit will help you to believe.

Lord God, help me to always be strong
and to think good things and to not allow
my mind to get stuck thinking bad things.

Amen.

I Will Make You New

"I will give them an undivided heart and put a new spirit in them; I will remove from them their heart of stone and give them a heart of flesh."

Ezekiel 11:19 (NIV)

- o - ∿∿ - - o -

I know you think that you can't change or that others can't change, but I can do anything. So, when you believe in Me, all of My power will change your heart and make everything in your spirit new.

So, if there is someone you know who needs Me, pray for them to open their heart to Me so that I can change them and make them new, too.

Dear God, remind me to pray for You to change my heart constantly. Help me to remember to pray for others' hearts, too.

Amen.

My Spirit Will Fill You

"Not by might nor by power, but by
My Spirit," says the LORD Almighty.

Zechariah 4:6 (NIV)

— o — ∿∿∿ — — o —

My Spirit within you will always fill you when you're feeling empty. But you must realize that you're feeling that way and come to Me for help.

Whatever I'm asking you to do—to be kind to those who hurt you, to love those who hate you—know that you cannot do this on your own. It's My Spirit within you that will do all of the work, you just need to surrender to Me and My help in whatever you're doing.

Lord, when I'm feeling empty, remind me that You are always with me and I can be kind even to those who are hurtful. I pray that Your Spirit will dwell in me and help me.

Amen.

I Will Fill You with Joy

Don't be lazy in showing your devotion.
Use your energy to serve the Lord.

Romans 12:11 (GW)

— o — ∿ — — o —

I know that on some days you might feel really empty and alone, but if you'll stay focused on Me, I will use My Spirit to make your sadness go away and I will give you faith to believe in all of the promises I've made you.

I don't want you to allow all of the bad things in your life to drag you down. Turn to Me and I will lift you up. It's My Spirit in you that will make you feel full of joy and fully alive, even when the things in life are bringing you down.

Dear God, help me to work hard at doing the things that You want me to do in my life. Fill me with Your Spirit so that I will be full of life and strength to fulfill Your purposes.

Amen.

When You're Feeling Empty...

You will rely on the Holy Spirit
to fill you with truth.

ROMANS 9:1

You will receive the Spirit
that God gives you that fills you with
power, love and self-discipline.

2 TIMOTHY 1:7

You will be thankful that
God has given you a new
heart and filled you with His Spirit.

EZEKIEL 11:19

You will call upon the Holy Spirit to fill
you with strength, peace, and joy.

ZECHARIAH 4:6

You will continue to work hard at
doing the things you're supposed to
do in life, fulfilling God's purpose.

ROMANS 12:11

What I've learned this week about feeling empty...

_____

_____

_____

_____

_____

_____

_____

_____

_____

_____

_____

_____

_____

_____

_____

_____

Just Follow Me

Jesus called out to them, "Come, follow Me,
and I will show you how to fish for people!"

Matthew 4:19

— o — ∿ — — o —

There will be days when you wonder why you're even on earth. I know that sometimes it feels like you don't have a purpose. But the purpose you can always be sure of is that you're to lead others to Me.

That doesn't mean I want you to preach everywhere you go. I just want you to live the life I've asked you to, being loving, kind, and full of joy so that others can see Me in you. Just follow Me.

Lord, sometimes I don't know what I'm doing in life and I need to know that You have purposes for Me. Help me to hear Your voice and listen to Your plan for me.

Amen.

I Will Tell You

Do not *merely* look out for your own personal
interests, but also for the interests of others.

Philippians 2:4 (AMP)

- o - ∿∿∿ — - o -

One of the main reasons I've given you life and put
you on earth is so that you can help others. So, I
want you to focus on looking out for others because
you know that I AM looking out for you.

I will always lead and guide you and open your eyes
to see what others need around you; but it's up to
you to use the life I've given you. I will give you all
you need to help others.

Dear God, open my eyes so that I can see how I can
help others. Use my life to be a blessing to those in need.
Amen.

I Am Your Perfect Example

"I have given you an example to follow.
Do as I have done to you."

John 13:15

— o — ∿ — — o —

You might think it's too hard to live the life I want you to. You probably think you have to be perfect, but you don't. I will never ask you to be perfect. I just ask you to follow Jesus.

You won't always do things right, but I will always forgive you and help you to do anything I ask of you. Your purpose in life is to follow Jesus and I will do the rest.

Heavenly Father, I want to live the life You have planned for me...helping others and leading them to You.

Amen.

Love Those Around You

If someone has enough money to live well and sees
a brother or sister in need but shows no compassion—
how can God's love be in that person?

1 John 3:17

– o – ~~~ – – o –

Love is not just a feeling...it's a verb—love does
things. Since My Spirit lives in you and I have given
you My love, you will find yourself wanting to love
and help others.

I will always help you to see how you can be loving
and kind to those who really need someone to care
about them. You can be such a blessing to others,
and you should know that I will always take care of
you and look for ways to bless you as you love those
who need it.

Lord, fill my heart with Your love and
open my eyes to those who need my help.
Help me to be caring, loving, and kind.

Amen.

Give Generously

"Give, and it will be given to you. A good measure,
pressed down, shaken together and running over,
will be poured into your lap. For with the
measure you use, it will be measured to you."

Luke 6:38 (NIV)

- o - ~~~ - - o -

Sometimes when you pray, you only pray for what
you need. But I also want you to pray for things that
others need. I tell you in the Bible to give and I will
give to you—and that's a promise.

So, instead of focusing on the troubles in your life,
focus on others and how you can help them...give
to them and show My love for them. I just want you
to focus on giving and I will give you all you need
and more.

Heavenly Father, I pray that You will help
me to be loving and kind to others, just as
You've been loving and kind to me.

Amen.

TIME TO REFLECT

When You Don't Know Why You're Here...

You will remember that you're supposed to follow Jesus and you will pray for God's help in following Him.

MATTHEW 4:19

You will focus on the needs of others and realize that God wants you to help others.

PHILIPPIANS 2:4

You will be loving, kind, and giving to others, following God's example.

JOHN 13:15

You will look for ways to be helpful to others.

1 JOHN 3:17

You will ask God to open your eyes to the needs of others and ask Him in what way you can be helpful and giving.

LUKE 6:38

What I've learned this week about not knowing why I'm here ...

_____

_____

_____

_____

_____

_____

_____

_____

_____

_____

_____

_____

_____

_____

_____

Know That You Are Saved

Since, therefore, we have now been justified
by His blood, much more shall we be saved by
Him from the wrath of God.

Romans 5:9 (ESV)

— o — ∿ — — o —

I want you to understand that My love for you means that even though you make mistakes, I will always forgive you. You are saved from punishment. You can freely enter into heaven.

I sent Jesus to save you. He paid for your sins, the things you do wrong, so that you don't have to suffer. He suffered for you. So, I want you to live in the joy I've given you—I have saved you.

Lord God, thank You for Your great love
and for saving me from my sins and suffering.

Amen.

Remember, I've Given You Grace

He gives us more grace. That is why Scripture says:
"God opposes the proud but shows favor to the humble."

James 4:6 (NIV)

– o – 〜〜 – – o –

Don't forget that I've given you grace—it's My love even though you don't deserve it. It's My grace that gives you the hope of going to heaven.

So, you don't need to be perfect to go to heaven, you just need to believe in Me. It's your faith in Me and My Son, Jesus, that makes sure you'll go to heaven. So, you don't have to be scared when you die, because you won't really die—you will live forever with Me in heaven.

Heavenly Father, thank You for Your grace that saves me. Thank You that I don't have to be scared, but can be glad that I will spend forever in heaven with You.

Amen.

Believe in Jesus

My old self has been crucified with Christ. It is no longer I who live, but Christ lives in me. So I live in this earthly body by trusting in the Son of God, who loved me and gave Himself for me.

Galatians 2:20

― ๐ ― ᨆᨆᨆ ― ― ๐ ―

Whenever you choose to believe in Me, you are saying that you want to change and become who I want you to be. When you believe, My Spirit puts a new heart in you and the Spirit will help you to do the things that I want you to—to be loving, kind, and forgiving.

When you believe in Jesus, everything is new, including who you are. The old you is gone—now I live in you and one day you will live forever with Me in heaven.

Dear God, thank You for giving me a new heart and filling me with all that You are so that I can live a life where I am loving, kind, and forgiving.

Amen.

Know That Jesus Saves

Therefore He is able, once and forever, to save those who come to God through Him. He lives forever to intercede with God on their behalf.

Hebrews 7:25

– o – ∿ – – o –

When I save you from your sins, I just need to save you once. Once you are saved, you are completely saved.

When you make mistakes, you should still come to Me to be forgiven. But even though you mess up, you remain saved. I know you cannot be perfect, but I AM and I will always help you when you come to Me.

Heavenly Father, thank You for saving me so that I don't have to suffer for my sins and I can live with You forever.

Amen.

Remember, My Love Saves

Come and see for yourself.

John 1:46

– o – ∿∿ – – o –

My love saves everyone, but it has a special way to save just you. I have a plan that I've had all along to show you who Jesus is and how He died for you on the Cross.

And then, My plan for you also includes you telling and showing others who Jesus is and helping them to see that they can be saved too.

Lord, help me to lead others to Jesus so that they can know You for themselves and live with You forever in heaven.

Amen.

TIME TO REFLECT

When You Want to Know About Heaven...

You will be thankful that
God has saved you and
you don't have to suffer for your sins.

ROMANS 5:9

You will be thankful for the grace God has given
you to save you so that you can go to heaven.

JAMES 4:6

You will remember that the old you is gone
and you have been saved by Jesus so that
you can live the life God wants you to.

GALATIANS 2:20

You will be full of faith and be thankful
that God has saved you so you can
live in heaven forever with Him.

HEBREWS 7:25

You will help others to know Jesus so that they
can be saved and go to heaven, too.

JOHN 1:46

What I've learned this week about heaven...

DAY 309

Go to My Word

"You will know the truth, and the truth will set you free."

John 8:32 (GW)

— o — ⌁ — — o —

I know it's hard to tell sometimes what is the truth and what is a lie, but the Bible can help you because it is filled with truth.

It's My Word, the Bible, that helps you to know what is right or wrong and what it is I want you to do. Lies in the world can make you feel trapped and it's My Truth, in My Word, that will set you free.

Heavenly Father, thank You for setting me free from all the lies in the world by giving me the truth through Your Word.

Amen.

The Bible Will Guide You

They delight in the law of the LORD,
meditating on it day and night.

Psalm 1:2

— o — ∿∿ — — o —

If you just read the Bible every once in a while, you won't know all that it has to say and you won't be able to always know what is the truth or a lie until it is sometimes too late.

So, I want you to read and think about My Word all the time, day and night. When you are constantly thinking about My Word, the Truth sits in your heart and mind, and then when you need help, My Word will lead and guide you.

Lord, thank You for the Bible that leads and guides me in the way I should go. Help me to focus on Your Word.

Amen.

The Bible Is Your Guidepost

Great peace have those who love Your law,
and nothing can make them stumble.

Psalm 119:165 (NIV)

$- o - \sim\sim -- o -$

Do you know what it's like to trip and fall? Of course you do...sometimes it scares you, sometimes you get hurt. The same thing happens in life, but the Bible can keep you from stumbling so much.

When you use My Word to help you in life, to know what is right and wrong, to know what is truth or lie, you won't fall so much.

Heavenly Father, thank You for helping me when I do things wrong or get confused. Help me to look to You for help.

Amen.

Let Me Change the Way You Think

Don't copy the behavior and customs of this world, but let God transform you into a new person by changing the way you think. Then you will learn to know God's will for you, which is good and pleasing and perfect.

Romans 12:2

— o — ∿ — - o —

I know it's easy to just "go along with the crowd", but sometimes that will get you in trouble...and I want you to have a joyful life.

It's when you read My Word that you will learn what is right and wrong. Others, even adults, will tell you lies and try to hurt you—sometimes you won't even realize it because they are lies and lies are tricky. But My Word helps you to see clearly what is truth.

Lord God, I need You to transform my heart and help me to think straight. It's easy to just do what others are doing, but I want to only do what You want me to do.

Amen.

Stay Focused on Me

So prepare your minds for action and exercise self-control. Put all your hope in the gracious salvation that will come to you when Jesus Christ is revealed to the world.

1 Peter 1:13

Life can be really confusing because life is hard and there are a lot of lies. So, I want you to stay focused on Me, so that you can think right.

When you're angry, sad, or lonely, things can seem one way, when they really aren't, so it's the Bible that will help you when you're feeling this way so that you are not confused and always know that I'm here to help you.

Dear God, sometimes I get confused, sad and lonely. Fill my mind and my heart with Your Word so that I can be strong and full of hope.

Amen.

TIME TO REFLECT

When You Want to Know the Truth...

You will rely on God's Word, the Bible, to help you know what is the truth, so that you won't fall into the trap of lies.

JOHN 8:32

You will keep your mind focused on God's Word all of the time.

PSALM 1:2

You will be thankful that God's Word keeps you living the life He wants you to and you will focus on Him.

PSALM 119:165

You won't do what everyone else is doing... you will do only what God wants you to do and you'll ask Him for help.

ROMANS 12:2

You will keep your mind focused on God's Truth in His Word and ask Him to help you not to be confused.

1 PETER 1:13

What I've learned this week about knowing the truth...

_____

_____

_____

_____

_____

_____

_____

_____

_____

_____

_____

_____

_____

_____

_____

_____

_____

I Am Your Hiding Place

You are my hiding place; You protect me from
trouble. You surround me with songs of victory.

Psalm 32:7

- o - ∿∿ - - o -

When you are frightened or afraid, you can hide with
Me. I AM your hiding place. I have promised to protect you at all times and in all ways.

So, I need you to run to Me when you don't know
what to do. I AM with you every step of the way. I
will help you to fight all of your battles. I just want
you to be at peace and trust Me all of the time.

Heavenly Father, thank You for protecting me and letting
me hide with You, so that I can feel loved and safe.

Amen.

Cry Out to Me

I cried out to the LORD in my great
trouble, and He answered me.

Jonah 2:2

I know sometimes you might not think I'm listening,
especially when you are in trouble...when nothing is
changing. When your heart is breaking and you're
scared and afraid, I will rescue you.

When you're in trouble, cry out to Me and I will answer you. It might not happen right away, but I will
help you in My perfect way and perfect time.

Lord, sometimes I feel so afraid and I don't feel like anyone
can help me. I am thankful that I can run to You for help.
Amen.

Always Have Hope

As for me, I will always have hope;
I will praise You more and more.

Psalm 71:14 (NIV)

– o – ∿∿ – – o –

I know that when you're in trouble, it can feel like there is no hope, but there is always hope because I AM God.

When things are hard, you need to continue to pray and have hope. If you're trying to put your hope in anything other than Me, you will be disappointed. So keep reading My Word and praising Me for keeping My promises. There is nothing I can't do.

Heavenly Father, help me to always
have hope even when things seem
really bad and there's nothing I can do about it.

Amen.

DAY 319

I Hear Your Cries

I waited patiently for the LORD to help me,
and He turned to me and heard my cry.

Psalm 40:1

Everyone, at some point, needs to be rescued. Things go wrong, life is hard and there are things that you can't do. But I AM on your side and I AM here to help you.

So, when you call to Me, I will help you, but sometimes you must be patient. My plans and miracles don't always happen right away. So keep trusting Me, even when nothing is happening, My help is on the way.

Lord, thank You for rescuing me when I'm afraid and I don't know what to do. I AM so thankful for Your love and help.

Amen.

I Will Rescue You

Praise to the God of Shadrach, Meshach, and Abednego! He sent His angel to rescue His servants who trusted in Him.

Daniel 3:28

— o — ∿∿ — — o —

No matter what you are going through, you are never alone. Know that I AM always a prayer away from helping you. I AM always able to rescue you.

Even when you're struggling and feeling like nothing is happening, you should always know that I AM in control—even if things in life are not going well or getting better.

Heavenly Father, I am so thankful that You rescue me when life gets out of control. I pray that You will give me peace to know that You are always in control.

Amen.

TIME TO REFLECT

When You Need to Be Rescued...

You will run to God so
that He can protect you
from trouble and help you.

PSALM 32:7

You will cry out to God for help and know
that He will answer you.

JONAH 2:2

You will always have hope and
trust God more and more.

PSALM 71:14

You will wait patiently for God to help you and
trust that He hears your heart cry out to Him.

PSALM 40:1

You will praise God that
He rescues you because
you trust in Him at all times.

DANIEL 3:28

What I've learned
this week about being rescued...

_____

_____

_____

_____

_____

_____

_____

_____

_____

_____

_____

_____

_____

_____

_____

_____

_____

_____

I Am Here to Help

Therefore each of you must put off falsehood
and speak truthfully to your neighbor, for
we are all members of one body.

Ephesians 4:25 (NIV)

- o - ⌁ - - o -

There will always be things in your life that will make you angry. And sometimes being angry can make you sin and do wrong things. So, when you're angry, I need you to stop and pray so that I can help you with your anger.

I can help you see things differently and know that everything is going to be okay because I AM in control. So, know that I AM here to help you...even when you're angry.

Lord, help me to be truthful and speak kindly
of others even when I'm upset and angry.

Amen.

My Spirit Will Calm You

Don't be quick to get angry,
because anger is typical of fools.

Ecclesiastes 7:9 (GW)

– o – ∿ – – o –

Even though you might get angry sometimes, you shouldn't be angry all of the time. My Spirit within you will help you to be patient and loving and peaceful.

It's okay to feel angry. Anger can make you want to help others who are treated badly or be kind to someone who needs a friend. But I want you to rely on Me to help you calm your anger so that it does not control you in a bad way. I don't want anger to steal your joy.

Dear God, sometimes I get angry and I lose my peace. Please help me to have a quiet heart that is calm and joyful.

Amen.

Be the Calm in the Storm

A hot-tempered man stirs up strife, but he who
is slow to anger and patient calms disputes.

Proverbs 15:18 (AMP)

— o — ~~ — — o —

I don't want you looking for reasons to be angry. There are enough problems in life...I don't want you to be angry about everything all of the time.

The heart and mind I've given you is peaceful, patient, and loving. And even though sometimes you might experience the feeling of anger, I want you to learn to let go of your anger so it doesn't keep you from having the joyful life you're supposed to have.

Lord God, I get angry and want to get back at those who upset me. Help me to be peaceful and let things go.

Amen.

Trust Me with Your Hurt

But now is the time to get rid of anger, rage,
malicious behavior, slander, and dirty language.
Don't lie to each other, for you have stripped off
your old sinful nature and all its wicked deeds.

Colossians 3:8-9

— o — ∿ — — o —

There are some things in your life that you just need to get rid of. I know things and people can make you angry, but it ends up hurting you more than them.

I want you to come to Me when you're angry or someone has hurt you. I will help you to have peace instead of feeling anger and wanting revenge. I don't want you to try and get back at others and hurt them because they hurt you. I want you to trust Me to handle it all.

Heavenly Father, help me to release my anger
to You. Give me the strength to love others
instead of hating when I am hurt.

Amen.

DAY 327

Treat Others Well

"Do to others as you would like them to do to you."

Luke 6:31

- o - ∿∿ -- - o -

I know that sometimes others can be mean and hurt your feelings. But I don't want you to hurt them back. I want you to show them that you are Mine, that you have My heart and then maybe they will believe in Me too.

You should always treat others the way you want them to treat you. Don't allow anger or jealousy to steal your joy. Even when others are mean to you, just be nice to them.

Lord God, when others hurt me, help me to still be kind to them and come to You to heal my heart.

Amen.

TIME TO REFLECT

When You're Angry...

You will always speak kindly and let God
handle your hurting heart.

EPHESIANS 4:25

You will not be quick to get angry,
but will keep calm and ask God for
help with what is bothering you.

ECCLESIASTES 7:9

You will keep calm and
remember that God does
not want you to get angry.

PROVERBS 15:18

You will run to God for help and
get rid of all of your anger, bad behavior,
bad words and your wanting to get back
at those who hurt you.

COLOSSIANS 3:8-9

You will do to others as you
would like them to do to you.

LUKE 6:31

What I've learned this week about getting angry...

_____

_____

_____

_____

_____

_____

_____

_____

_____

_____

_____

_____

_____

_____

_____

Pray for Help Today

"Don't worry about tomorrow, for tomorrow will bring
its own worries. Today's trouble is enough for today."

Matthew 6:34

- o - ∿ - - o -

I don't want you wasting your time worrying about
tomorrow—you've got enough problems to deal
with today. So, I want you to focus on and pray about
"today", not tomorrow.

There are so many things in life that you can't control.
I want you to stay focused on Me and My power and
all I can do to help you. I can do the impossible.

Heavenly Father, help me to focus on
today and not worry about tomorrow.

Amen.

DAY 331

You're Guarded by Angels

He will put His angels in charge of you
to protect you in all your ways.

Psalm 91:11 (GW)

- o - ∿ - - o -

I AM always watching over you and you should know that My angels are watching over you too—all the time. So, I don't want you to worry, I want you to be at peace.

I want you to learn to have faith and to trust Me even when things seem really bad. When you're afraid and feeling all alone, I want you to come to Me in prayer and ask for My help. Then, wait patiently, knowing that I AM always loving you and protecting you.

Lord God, thank You for Your angels that are always
watching over me so that I can be at peace.

Amen.

I AM at Work in You

Because of His glory and excellence, He has given us great and precious promises. These are the promises that enable you to share His divine nature and escape the world's corruption caused by human desires.

2 Peter 1:4

- o - ~~ — - o -

I have made so many promises for your life—big and small, and I want you to know them all.

When you are afraid of the future, upset and worried, I want you to know I AM with you—right where you are. I AM always looking for ways to bless you, always at work, doing what is best for your life. But don't try to understand everything I AM doing, because you can't. Just trust that I AM in control and everything is going to be okay.

Dear God, I am so thankful for the promises
You've made me so that I can have hope
and trust You even when I don't understand.

Amen.

I Will Give You What You Need

He has shown kindness by giving you rain from heaven and crops in their seasons; He provides you with plenty of food and fills your hearts with joy.

Acts 14:17 (NIV)

- o - ∿∿ - - o -

I know sometimes you worry if you will have "enough". Enough friends, enough "things", but you need to remember that I have promised that you will always have enough. I know exactly what you need.

I promise you that My plans for your life are far better than anything you might have planned. So, I want you to learn to trust Me and be at peace that whatever you need I will give you.

Lord God, help me to be satisfied with what I have and know that You will always make sure I have "enough".
Amen.

Trust Me to Work Miracles

Then Moses stretched out his hand over the sea, and the
LORD drove the sea back by a strong east wind all night
and made the sea dry land, and the waters were divided.

Exodus 14:21 (ESV)

- o - ⌇⌇⌇ -- o -

Maybe you've read or heard when I split open the seas so that I could help people from evil and danger...it's the story of the Red Sea being parted. I want you to know about this because it shows you how powerful I AM, and how I can make miracles happen, even at the last minute.

So, just because things seem really bad and it doesn't look like things are going to get better, it doesn't mean that it will stay that way. I can do ANY-THING in the blink of an eye.

Heavenly Father, thank You for the Bible
that teaches me about Your love and power
and that You can do the impossible.

Amen.

TIME TO REFLECT

When You Need God's Care...

You will not worry about tomorrow.
You will give God all of your worries.

MATTHEW 6:34

You will be at peace knowing that God's angels
are always looking over you and will help you.

PSALM 91:11

You will cling to God's promises for you and
know that He will always take care of you.

2 PETER 1:4

You will be filled with joy because God
promises that you will always have enough.

ACTS 14:17

You will remember that God does the
impossible and He will always make sure
that everything is going to be okay.

EXODUS 14:21

What I've learned
this week about God's care...

Count them One by One

All praise to God, the Father of our Lord Jesus Christ, who has blessed us with every spiritual blessing in the heavenly realms because we are united with Christ.

Ephesians 1:3

I want you to always be thankful for what you have and realize that I AM always looking for ways to bless you.

While you're waiting for Me to answer prayers, I want you to look for ways that you can be a blessing to others. Every time I bless you, I AM giving you a little bit of heaven on earth. You can be a blessing to others and bring them a little heaven too.

Lord, help me to be a blessing to others and trust that You will take care of all of my needs.

Amen.

Know What You Really Need

You don't have what you want because
you don't ask God for it.

James 4:2

– o – ∿∿ – – o –

Sometimes you worry, get upset, and get frustrated that things aren't working out in your life, and sometimes that's because you haven't asked Me for what you want or need.

Even though I already know your wants and needs, getting closer to Me and knowing Me better means talking to Me and asking Me for things. Doing this makes your faith stronger and that's what you really need.

Heavenly Father, when I'm worried and upset, remind me to come to You and ask for what I need.

Amen.

Remember the Free Gift

The promise is received by faith.
It is given as a free gift.

Romans 4:16

— o — ∿ — — o —

There's really not much in your life that you will ever get for free, but My love for you and My promises to you are free...when you believe in Me and My Son, Jesus. There is nothing you have to do to earn My love and My promises. That is a blessing you can be thankful for.

When you feel empty, like nothing is going your way, I want you to stop and think about all of the good things in your life that I have given to you and realize that you should be thankful because they are free gifts.

Lord, thank You for Your promises. Thank You for being with me and giving me hope.

Amen.

Look for the Hidden Blessings Too

"Don't be afraid, for I am with you. Don't be discouraged, for I am your God. I will strengthen you and help you. I will hold you up with My victorious right hand."

Isaiah 41:10

— o — ⁓ — — o —

When life is hard, I know it seems like it's all My fault and you don't think I know what I'm doing. But sometimes I allow things to be hard so it gives your faith a chance to grow. When you have troubles, they are hidden blessings because they give you a chance to believe in Me more.

So, when troubles come, stop and remember that I've promised to work all things together for good.

Dear God, I know that sometimes I am not thankful when life is hard...help me to see that You are giving me stronger faith when there is trouble in my life.

Amen.

Trust Me to Do the Impossible

The LORD is good to those whose hope is
in Him, to the one who seeks Him.

Lamentations 3:25 (NIV)

– o – ∿∿ – – o –

When you're down and alone and sad, I want you
to count your blessings—focus on all of the good
things in your life. When life is hard, it's really easy
to lose hope, so I want you to keep thinking about
My promises.

Even when it seems like there is no hope, I want you
to trust Me and remember that I can do the impossible. There is always hope if you will pray to Me and
keep looking for Me to answer your prayers.

Heavenly Father, help me to count my
blessings and be thankful for the small things
in my life as well as the big things.

Amen.

TIME TO REFLECT

When You Need to Count Your Blessings...

You will be thankful for the blessings God gives to you.

EPHESIANS 1:3

You will remember to pray and ask God for what you want and need.

JAMES 4:2

You will thank God for His grace and His promises that are given to you when you believe and have faith.

ROMANS 4:16

You will not be afraid or discouraged, but will be strengthened by God who always helps you and blesses you.

ISAIAH 41:10

You will seek God and remember that He has promised to take care of you and bless you.

LAMENTATIONS 3:25

What I've learned this week about counting my blessings...

_____

_____

_____

_____

_____

_____

_____

_____

_____

_____

_____

_____

_____

_____

_____

_____

I Will Make You Well

The human spirit can endure in sickness,
but a crushed spirit who can bear?

Proverbs 18:14 (NIV)

- o - ∿ - - o -

Sometimes you get sick and wonder if you'll get better. I want you to know that I AM always looking after you and I can heal you.

When you are sick, I want you to pray for Me to heal you. I have all of the healing power you need to make you well. But while you're sick, spend time with Me and rest, knowing that while you're praying, I will make you well.

Lord God, I am so thankful that You take care of me
and that I can rest and know that You will heal me.

Amen.

I Will Heal Your Disease

Praise the LORD, my soul, and forget not all His benefits—
who forgives all your sins and heals all your diseases.

Psalm 103:2-3 (NIV)

I know when you're sick it may be difficult to believe that I care, but I AM always with you, always watching over you and I will take care of you and make you well again.

Just because you're not feeling well, I don't want you to get discouraged. I want you to learn that I can do all things...and that includes healing you.

Heavenly Father, I am so thankful that You are always watching over me and have promised to heal me. Help me to trust in You even though I'm not feeling well.

Amen.

Pray in Faith

The prayer offered in faith will make the sick
person well; the Lord will raise them up.

James 5:15 (NIV)

− o − ∿∿ − − o −

When you're sick, remember to pray. Believe that I will heal you. Your faith may not seem strong, but that's okay...you only need faith as small as a mustard seed.

When you have faith, I will give you hope. My promises can fill you with peace and help you rest as you wait on My healing. I want you to keep focused on Me even when you're in pain. Pray when you're in pain and trust Me to help you.

Lord God, I pray that You will heal me and that
You will heal others. I am thankful for the hope
and rest You give to me when I am sick.

Amen.

DAY 347

Rest Peacefully

I'll restore your health and heal your
wounds," declares the LORD.

Jeremiah 30:17 (GW)

— o — ∿ — — o —

When you break a bone, that bone becomes stronger. And when you're sick, and have to have faith, your faith grows stronger. So, when you're sick, rely on My promises that I will heal you.

Then, I want you to rest peacefully and have hope. There is nothing that I can't do, so I simply want you to believe. I can do miracles, so pray for them.

Heavenly Father, thank You for making my faith stronger
by using my sickness to bring me closer to You.

Amen.

There Will Be No More Pain

"He will wipe every tear from their eyes. There will be no more death or mourning or crying or pain, for the old order of things has passed away."

Revelation 21:4 (NIV)

— o — ∿ — — o —

I want you to know that one day, when you're in heaven, there will be no more pain and suffering. Your heart will not be broken and your body will never be sick.

So, when you're not feeling well, I want you to stay focused on Me and My promise to heal you. Don't allow your pain and frustration to get in the way of believing in My healing power. I never lie. I want you to focus on one thing: My promises for you and My love for you.

Lord God, I look forward to the day when I am with You in heaven and there will be no more sickness, but I am thankful that You love me and will heal me when I am sick on earth.

Amen.

TIME TO REFLECT

When You're Sick...

You will look to God for healing and you
will have hope and be at peace.

EXODUS 14:21

You will praise God who forgives all
of your sins and heals you.

PSALM 103:2-3

You will rely on God's promise that if
you pray the sick will be made well.

JAMES 5:15

You will trust that God has promised to heal you.

JEREMIAH 30:17

You will look forward to heaven where there
will be no more crying and no more sickness.

REVELATION 21:4

What I've learned this week about being sick...

Shine My Light For Others

Since God chose you to be the holy people He loves, you must clothe yourselves with tenderhearted mercy, kindness, humility, gentleness, and patience.

Colossians 3:12

− o − ∿ − − o −

I know sometimes life is confusing and you're not really sure what you're supposed to be doing, but there is always one thing that I want you to remember to do—be a light to those living in this dark world.

Others need to know Jesus too, and you can lead them to Him by being loving and kind. So, when you're not sure what to do with your faith, know that you can always be a bright shining light.

Heavenly Father, help me to be a light to others and lead them to You so they will know Your amazing love and grace.
Amen.

Be What I Created You to Be

My message and my preaching were very plain.
Rather than using clever and persuasive speeches,
I relied only on the power of the Holy Spirit.

1 Corinthians 2:4

— o — ∿∿ — — o —

Because you have faith in Me it does not mean that I want you to go around preaching all of the time. Others will see your faith in Me by what you say and do.

So, I want you to pray that the Holy Spirit will work in you and help you to pray for others and lead them to Me by just being who I've created you to be. If you'll just allow Me to work through you to reach others, you'll find yourself bringing a little heaven to earth.

Lord, open my eyes to the needs of others and to pray for them to come to You so that they might receive Your grace when they need it.

Amen.

Cling to Your Faith

As for you, be strong and do not give up,
for your work will be rewarded.

2 Chronicles 15:7 (NIV)

- o - ～～ - - o -

I know that sometimes faith is really hard. You try really hard to say and do the right things, but you're not sure if you're doing things well.

I want you to know that My Spirit will always help you. You don't need to try and do everything on your own. I will always lead and guide you and help you to know what to do. When you're weak, I will carry you and if you do not give up, I will reward you.

Dear God, help me to be strong and not give up in my faith, even when life is really hard. Please lead and guide me when I don't know what to do.

Amen.

Serve with Strength

Whoever speaks must speak God's words. Whoever serves must serve with the strength God supplies so that in every way God receives glory through Jesus Christ. Glory and power belong to Jesus Christ forever and ever! Amen.

1 Peter 4:11 (GW)

─ o ─ ∿∿ ─ ─ o ─

You were put on the earth for big reasons. The most important reason is to help others learn about Me. When you look for ways to help others, when you are kind and giving, you are helping others to see Me.

Each and every day, even when things are not going just right in your life, I want you to be strong and serve others by paying attention to their needs. I want you to always believe what I've promised to you—I will give you all you need and more.

Heavenly Father, help me to be strong and speak Your words, even when it feels uncomfortable. Open my eyes to helping others around me to see who You are.

Amen.

Know That I Chose You

"Go! I've chosen this man
to bring My name to nations,
to kings, and to the people."

Acts 9:15 (GW)

- o - ~~~ - - o -

I know that sometimes you feel like you don't have what it takes to help others to see Jesus. But if you will just pray to Me for help, My Spirit will do all the work.

I will fill you with wisdom that tells you what to do and I will give you love in your heart to do what must be done. It might be helping a friend or being kind to someone who has no friends. But don't be afraid...I have chosen you and I will help you.

Lord God, thank You for choosing me to help
You love others. Give me the strength and
faith to do what You want me to do.

Amen.

TIME TO REFLECT

When You're Not Sure What God Wants ...

You will be tenderhearted' showing, mercy, kindness, humility, gentleness, and patience because of God's love for you.

COLOSSIANS 3:12

You will ask the Holy Spirit to lead and guide you in bringing others to Jesus.

1 CORINTHIANS 2:4

You will be strong and not give up in doing what God asks you to do in life and know that He has promised to reward you for your faith.

2 CHRONICLES 15:7

You will speak God's Word that has power and is able to change hearts and heal the sick. You will rely on His love and power to do what He calls you to do.

1 PETER 4:11

You will be thankful that God has chosen you to help Him reach the lost.

ACTS 9:15

What I've learned this week about God's will...

There Is Power in Me

I did this so you would trust not in human
wisdom but in the power of God.

1 Corinthians 2:5

— ○ — ⌁ — — ○ —

So many times you think that things can't be done because you think My power is like human power— but humans can't do miracles, only I can.

When you're dealing with tough things in life and you're feeling like nothing is going your way, remember that I have promised to help you and I have unlimited power. So, you don't have to worry or be afraid. All you need to do is trust in Me and continue to pray.

Heavenly Father, thank You for always taking care
of me. I am so grateful for Your power that does
miracles and can help me when all hope seems lost.

Amen.

Know Who I Am

Who is a God like You?
You forgive sin
and overlook the rebellion
of Your faithful people.

Micah 7:18 (GW)

— ○ — ∿∿ — — ○ —

When you wonder who I AM, know that I AM the One and only God that makes all things possible. I can do miracles in the blink of an eye and change everything.

I want you to have faith in who I AM and not doubt when things are hard or people hurt you. I AM always within you, changing you, building your faith, and making miracles that you will one day see. So, don't try to handle life on your own, you need Me because I AM God and I can do anything and everything.

Lord God, I praise You for who You are...Your love and Your grace are all I will ever need.

Amen.

My Name Is a Strong Tower

The name of the LORD is a strong tower;
the righteous man runs into it and is safe.

Proverbs 18:10 (ESV)

- o - ~~~ – - o -

There is great power that comes out of heaven when you call upon My name. When you come to Me, I can help you in every way that you need Me to.

When things are going really badly and you feel like the whole world is against you, you need to remember that I AM always with you and will always help you. Just call on Me and I'll be there.

Dear God, help me to remember that coming to You is the best thing I can do and praying in the name of Jesus works miracles because of Your love and Your power.

Amen.

Know You're on the Winning Side

Thanks be to God, who gives us the victory
through our Lord Jesus Christ.

1 Corinthians 15:57 (ESV)

– o – ∿ – – o –

You can't always win at everything in life, but if you trust in Me, you will win...in the end.

I need you to believe that My power can save you—no matter what the situation is...no matter how hard things might be. When you're doubting, go to the Bible and look at all of the promises I've made you. You can keep going and be strong because I will always give you strength.

Lord, thank You for helping me to win in life.
Thank You for the peace in Your promises
that assures me that You will save me.

Amen.

Try to Make Wise Decisions

God arms me with strength.
His perfect way sets me free.

2 Samuel 22:33 (GW)

- o - ∿∿ — - o -

Sometimes, when life gets hard, it might seem like things are out of control, but they are never out of My control. I make all the decisions. I decided how many stars are in the sky. I control everything.

So, when you're feeling like life is out control, remember that I control everything and I can do anything. Don't worry or be afraid...everything is going to be okay.

Dear God, thank You for helping me in every way so that I don't have to worry and I can rest and just trust You.

Amen.

TIME TO REFLECT

When You Feel Like the World Is Against You...

You will trust not in human
wisdom but in the power of God.

1 CORINTHIANS 2:5

You will know who God is. He forgives sin and
overlooks the rebellion of His faithful people.

MICAH 7:18

You will remember that the name of the
Lord is a strong tower; the righteous
man runs into it and is safe.

PROVERBS 18:10

You will thank God, who gives us the victory
through our Lord Jesus Christ.

1 CORINTHIANS 15:57

You will know that God arms you with strength.
His perfect way sets you free.

2 SAMUEL 22:33

What I've learned this week about feeling like the world is against you...

TIME TO REFLECT ON THE YEAR

Scripture verses that have meant the most to me:

_____

_____

_____

_____

_____

_____

_____

_____

_____

_____

_____

_____

_____

_____

_____

_____

_____